DATE			

89011622

MEDIA MANUALS

Effective TV Production

Gerald
Millerson

A Focal Press Book

Communication Arts Books
HASTINGS HOUSE, PUBLISHERS
New York, NY 10016

ISBN 8038-7163-5

*To my friends and colleagues of the
Department of Radio – Television – Film,
School of Communications and Theater,
Temple University, Philadelphia, Pa.*

Printed and Bound in Great Britain by Staples Printers Ltd, Kettering Northants

Contents

Introduction

Once we have overcome the initial awkwardness of unfamiliarity, we tend to take TV technicalities for granted. TV directing appears deceptively simple. Even junior schools compile their own video-recorded projects nowadays! The rawest beginner can hang a mike round someone's neck, point a camera at him, and zoom in and out!

But amateurish treatment soon loses its cuteness, and becomes a bore. Our audience grows frustrated, confused, even reduced to laughter – but in the wrong places. They become over-aware of mechanics, and inevitably compare the results with regular TV presentations seen at home.

It is seldom sufficient merely to *see* and *hear* the subject. How we *present* it is all important. And here lies the difference between the amateur and the professional. To use facilities imaginatively, conveying ideas clearly and persuasively, is a matter of know-how. And know-how can be learned. The trouble for the newcomer is that there seems such a lot to *be* learned.

This book has been written to help you acquire knowledge of important fundamentals quickly and to provide a firm foundation for experience. It outlines techniques and hazards of TV production and tells you how to organise your show in the most effective ways.

Contrary to widespread belief, the camera and microphone do not readily substitute for an on-the-spot observer. It is up to us to choose how and what these tools select, to suit our particular purposes. If we do this successfully, the results will be so obviously 'right', that our audience accepts them unquestioningly. Inappropriately used, the medium can get in the way of our message. Our audience can become distracted, misled – or go on to think about other things!

TV directing is always concerned with four basic issues:

The message. The programme material. What we are trying to say to our audience. The emotions we hope to engender in them.

The mechanics. The equipment we have available. What it can and can't do.

The methods. The techniques we choose to enable us to build up an arresting, interesting presentation.

The organisation. The behind-the-scenes activities that interrelate and coordinate the work of the production team.

This is our field of study.

Acknowledgement

The author would like to thank the Director of Engineering of The British Broadcasting Corporation for permission to publish this book.

9

Controlling a TV Production

Exactly what a TV director does varies between organisations and with the kind of programme material he is handling. He may be totally responsible for all the business and presentational aspects of the show, in a combined role of producer and director. Alternatively, he may concentrate on the creative side of the production, and leave administration to a producer. But whatever the job emphasis, we find the director the key figure in the studio production team, guiding, co-relating and unifying their efforts.

Typical directing roles

In a *presentational role,* the director presents for the screen a series of separate items or 'stories' devised by an editorial group. This is a common practice in current affairs, news, magazine programmes.

In a *selective role,* the director heads a team of specialists. After preliminary briefing or planning, they contribute their respective interpretations of his project (staging, lighting, costume, make-up, graphics, etc.). He appraises their treatments, and indicates any changes he feels necessary. The director himself concentrates on the dynamics of talent performance, camera operation and switching (editing).

In the role of an *originator,* the director may have devised the entire production concept. He will have written the script, and often initiated the staging treatment. His team of specialists translates the director's decisions into material terms. They organise the mechanics or construction required, costing and labour.

The organisational centre

Most people think of the TV director as the person in the production control room, heading his production team – the hub of the production operations. But this is only part of his job, albeit the major part. Underlying the work here, we have the important preliminaries of choosing and interpreting the programme subject, the organisation and planning. There is the selection of talent, discussion of treatment methods and equipment with specialists, research, pre-studio rehearsals, devising models perhaps, and the anticipation of the thousand and one facets that go to make up the total show. Contributory aspects do not just *appear*! The director sees that there is a need for a film clip here, a graphic there, an action prop or a certain mood to be created in a scene. His team of specialists and assistants help him achieve these, as near as possible to his ideal. But the director has initiated and evaluated their contributions. From the preliminary idea to the edited product, the director is the architect of his production – for which he ultimately accepts the responsibility.

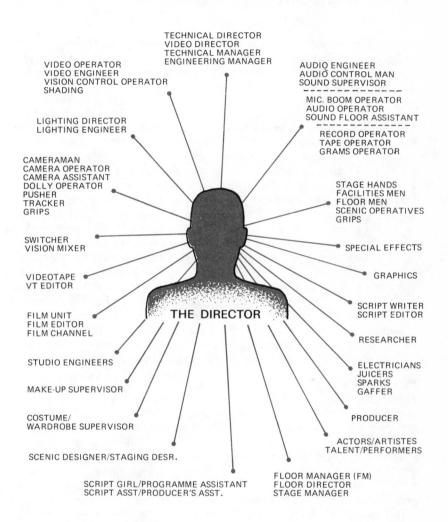

TECHNICAL DIRECTOR
VIDEO DIRECTOR
TECHNICAL MANAGER
ENGINEERING MANAGER

VIDEO OPERATOR
VIDEO ENGINEER
VISION CONTROL OPERATOR
SHADING

AUDIO ENGINEER
AUDIO CONTROL MAN
SOUND SUPERVISOR
– – – – – – – – – – – – –
MIC. BOOM OPERATOR
AUDIO OPERATOR
SOUND FLOOR ASSISTANT
– – – – – – – – – – – – – –
RECORD OPERATOR
TAPE OPERATOR
GRAMS OPERATOR

LIGHTING DIRECTOR
LIGHTING ENGINEER

CAMERAMAN
CAMERA OPERATOR
CAMERA ASSISTANT
DOLLY OPERATOR
PUSHER
TRACKER
GRIPS

STAGE HANDS
FACILITIES MEN
FLOOR MEN
SCENIC OPERATIVES
GRIPS

SWITCHER
VISION MIXER

SPECIAL EFFECTS

VIDEOTAPE
VT EDITOR

GRAPHICS

THE DIRECTOR

SCRIPT WRITER
SCRIPT EDITOR

FILM UNIT
FILM EDITOR
FILM CHANNEL

RESEARCHER

STUDIO ENGINEERS

ELECTRICIANS
JUICERS
SPARKS
GAFFER

MAKE-UP SUPERVISOR

COSTUME/
WARDROBE SUPERVISOR

PRODUCER

SCENIC DESIGNER/STAGING DESR.

ACTORS/ARTISTES
TALENT/PERFORMERS

SCRIPT GIRL/PROGRAMME ASSISTANT
SCRIPT ASST/PRODUCER'S ASST.

FLOOR MANAGER (FM)
FLOOR DIRECTOR
STAGE MANAGER

PRODUCTION TEAM

Studio Production Group
Studio production requires the services and skills of a large number of people.
Their exact job functions and titles vary between organisations.

A Studio Tour

TV systems today take many forms. They range from impressively equipped installations housing all the latest electronic wizardry, to modest self-contained one-man mobile units. Yet the production principles discussed here apply to them all.

TV studio
At first sight, the empty TV studio is a deceptively uncluttered, open area. But considerable care has gone into its design. Acoustically treated for optimum sound quality, its smooth, carefully levelled floor permits widespread camera movement. Apart from a *safety lane (fire lane)* around its edge, most of the studio floor is taken up by the *setting area (staging area)*. Here the prefabricated *scenery (staging)* is erected to form *settings* within which the action takes place (action areas). Quiet but powerful ventilation systems maintain a comfortable working temperature, despite the heat generated by equipment and lighting.

Studio lighting is provided by a series of special purpose lights hung individually, from *battens (barrels, bars)*, or clamped to a ceiling framework *(lighting grid)*, or on floor stands, or in ground units. Each provides illumination of carefully adjusted brightness and direction, to suit both the technical and artistic requirements of the production.

Around the walls we find the various technical appurtenances of studio equipment: power supplies, camera-cable sockets, controls for lighting equipment (hoists, switching), scenic hoists, etc.

TV cameras
Within the studio, the TV cameras (two to four are typical) are affixed to the top of mobile mountings (usually *pedestals,* page 18). A long attached cable connects each to a wall socket, and so to its associated video apparatus elsewhere. Although this 'umbilical cord' can cause snarl-ups or entanglements as cameras move around, supplies must be made to the camera, and the TV *video* (picture) signal taken from it. After suitable amplification and correction by a *video engineer (vision operator, shader)*, each camera's picture is fed to a *video switching (desk switcher, vision mixer)* in the nearby *production control room* (page 14). Here the director and his team sit, selecting from the cameras' shots and other picture sources (film, videotape, slides, remotes, etc.).

Ancillary rooms
Near the studio is the *scenery bay* or *storage area* which holds scenery and 'props' ready for productional use, and the *technical storage area* where technical equipment is kept, such as cameras, sound booms, picture monitors and loudspeakers, leaving the studio floor clear of surplus gear. A *preparation room* is sometimes available too, to set up experiments for science demonstrations, and make working models.

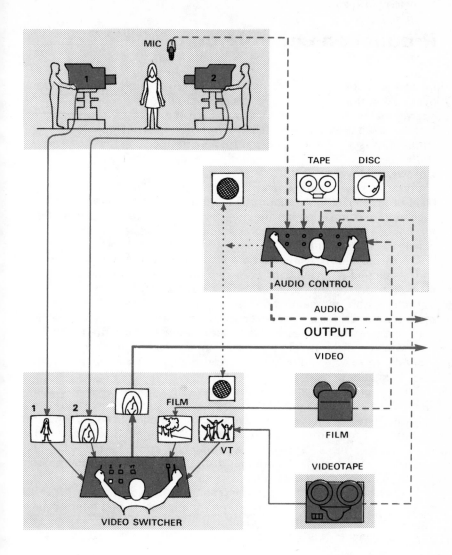

THE TV STUDIO SYSTEM

Basic Studio Layout

The cameras and other picture sources, are fed into the video switching unit (vision mixer) for selection. The audio pick-up too, is selected, controlled, monitored and distributed. The studio's audio and video outputs can be transmitted (live) or videorecorded.

Production Control Room

In one wall of the studio, beyond a large possibly tinted window overlooking the staging area, is the *production control room.* This is the operations centre of the TV show, where the director, his production staff, and contributory specialists work. Two layout approaches are commonly used in production control area design.

Communal layout
The first is a communal open plan arrangement. This may be in single level or split level form. Along the central desk sit the director and his assistant, accompanied by the *switcher (vision mixer), technical director, audio engineer* and *lighting director.* Job names and functions vary considerably (page 11).

On the row of *preview (channel) monitors* facing the desk are the various picture sources. Each camera's output, any film and videotape, slide scanners, remote sources, is displayed for continual monitoring. At the appropriate moment, the director (or a specialist *switcher, vision mixer* or the *technical director* himself) operates the *video switching unit,* and switches the selected picture to the studio output. This picture, which is displayed on the *master (main channel; line transmission) monitor,* can be fed to video recording equipment and/or transmitted 'live' as required.

The programme's audio contribution is controlled by a specialist, who switches, fades and blends the various sound sources from his console. Here he adjusts sound dynamics and quality to suit artistic and technical requirements. These audio sources include studio microphones, discs, audio tapes (reel, cassettes, cartridges), film, videotape, remotes, etc. Sometimes a small *announce booth* is included nearby, for announcements or commentaries.

In this communal layout, all personnel wear headsets in order to communicate with the crew, the programme itself being heard over a nearby loudspeaker. This can result in a fair amount of extraneous talk as all participants overhear everyone's instructions, cues, exchanges.

Sectionalised layout
Here the control area is divided into three rooms: *production control* in which the director, switcher (vision mixer) and technical director are located, a *sound control room,* and a *vision control room* (lighting and video control). The talkback system includes a communal (general) circuit continually relaying the director's information to the floor crew and adjacent control rooms. But individual specialists might have private-wire intercom circuits, to prevent their disrupting general talkback.

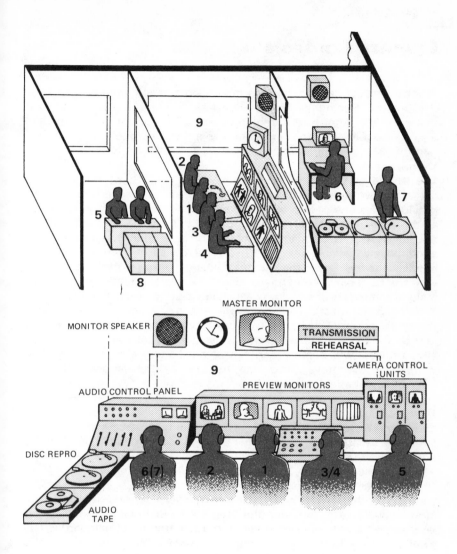

MASTER MONITOR

MONITOR SPEAKER

TRANSMISSION
REHEARSAL

9

CAMERA CONTROL UNITS

AUDIO CONTROL PANEL

PREVIEW MONITORS

DISC REPRO

AUDIO TAPE

6(7) 2 1 3/4 5

PRODUCTION NERVE CENTRE

Production Control Room Area

(A) In the *sectionalised* control area, the production control, audio control, and video control functions are located in separate rooms, to prevent interaction.
(B) In a *communal* control room layout, all the jobs are located around the director on a central desk.
1. Director.   2. Director's assistant.   3. Switcher/vision mixer.   4. Technical director (TM).   5. Video/engineer (shader), vision operator.   6. Audio/sound control.   7. Disc/audio-tape operator.   8. Lighting control.   9. Window to studio beyond.

Camera Controls

What engineers call the 'camera head', most people refer to simply as the *camera.* Behind its lens (or lenses), is the camera tube(s) that generates the TV picture (video), together with associated circuitry, and a small viewfinder for the cameraman to arrange his shot.

Camera lens
The simplest TV camera has a single fixed lens. Some monochrome cameras have several such lenses, fitted into a rotating *lens turret.* This provides a variety of lens angles (page 20). A handle (or push-buttons) at the rear of the camera head, rotates this turret to select the one needed. Nowadays, a single *zoom lens* is more often fitted. Its angle is continuously variable (page 26), altered by a control on a panning handle used to support the camera. The angular range of the zoom lens varies with design. A change of 5°–50° is typical. Some zoom lenses include *converters* or *extenders* which increase the available range.

Any camera must usually be re-focused as distance changes, to keep the subject sharp. On simpler cameras focus is adjusted by a ring on the lens barrel. More advanced cameras use a focus knob at the side of the camera head, while some zoom lenses have a rotating sleeve attached to a pan bar. Whatever the design, smooth unobtrusive focus-following is essential for effective camerawork.

Camera head
The *camera head* is attached to its mounting (usually a *tripod* or *pedestal)* by a *panning head.* This enables the camera to be *tilted* up and down, or *panned* (pivoted round) over a wide arc. A *pan bar* (or handle) is used to steady and guide the head movement.

The camera viewfinder shows a monochrome picture (even on colour cameras) of the shot taken in by the camera lens. A hood shields it from stray light, and a built-in magnifier, and electronic 'crispening' or enhancing assist focusing. When a camera has been selected by the switcher (page 44), a small indicator beside the viewfinder, and a numbered red *tally light (cue-light)* on top of the camera are illuminated.

The cameraman can often superimpose another camera's shot on his own viewfinder image *(mixed feeds),* so that the two pictures can be matched: e.g. to fit his shot of titling on to another camera's shot of a map.

Depending on the control room layout used (page 14), the cameraman's headset either intercommunicates with a communal (omnibus) intercom system, or he hears the director's talkback alone, together with the studio's audio output *(programme sound).* He can, when called, speak via private-wire circuits to the video engineer, lighting, or director.

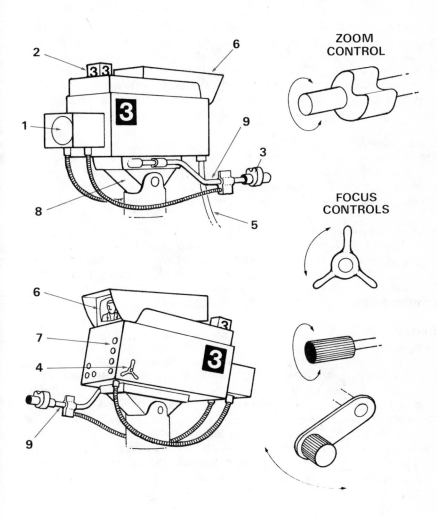

ZOOM
CONTROL

FOCUS
CONTROLS

TELEVISION CAMERA

Television Camera Features
Left, typical features.   Right zoom and focus controls.
1. Zoom lens.   2. Tally (cue) light, illuminated when the camera is selected.
3. Zoom control, adjusts lens-angle.   4. Focus control.   5. Camera cable
(video, electronics, and talkback circuits).   6. Viewfinder.   7. Shot box (where
fitted); press buttons select specific lens angles.   8. Panning (friction) head.
9. Panning handle.

Camera's Mounting

It is seldom practicable to hold even special lightweight TV cameras for any length of time. A shoulder harness helps, but precise camerawork is difficult, particularly for long-duration shots or when using narrower lens angles (page 24). Although the picture quality from lightweight cameras does not equal that from regular studio models, they are highly mobile and useful for tight corners. But for most applications, the TV camera is placed on a special mounting, giving firm, stable support.

Static mounting
Occasionally, the camera may be attached by its panning head to a suitably rigid structure nearby (eg: tubular scaffolding), or a simple *tripod* mounting. Very lightweight, but static, the tripod is invaluable on rough, uneven ground, or where safety requires complete immobility.

Rolling tripod
The *rolling tripod* (wheeled tripod) is the simplest mobile mounting. It comprises a tripod of prefixed working height, on a castored base *(skid).* It is suitable for movement between, rather than during shots. It is, however, quite satisfactory for less demanding production treatment, or semi-static situations, particularly where portability is essential.

Pedestal
The *pedestal* or 'ped' is undoubtedly the most widely used studio mounting, and operationally the most flexible. It enables the cameraman to alter camera height and/or position smoothly and quite quickly, even when on shot. For this, it needs a flat, level, uncluttered floor. Its height can be altered rapidly, or almost imperceptibly between its limits (1·1–1·5 m, $3\frac{1}{2}$ to 5 ft are typical), and can be left at any intermediate height. Pedestal moves can be subtly controlled, but one cannot expect the camerman to push his pedestal around rapidly and accurately at maximum or minimum heights. Particularly where older, heavier pedestal units are used, the cameraman may need help for more complex moves.

Camera dollies
For the most elaborate, closely-controlled camerawork *camera dollies* are used. Instead of the cameraman having to adjust all camera operations himself, some can be carried out by an assistant. As the cameraman may need to focus, compose his shot, adjust lens angle, alter camera height, and push and guide his pedestal simultaneously, the need for dollies during complicated treatment is evident – particularly for wide height variations. Dollies may be controlled manually or electrically.

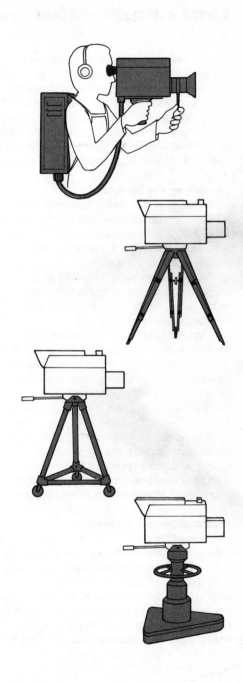

The hand-held camera
Supported by a shoulder harness, the hand-held camera is attached to a back-pack (transmitter or videorecorder).

The tripod
A static mounting, providing a firm, stable base for the camera – particularly on uneven ground.

The rolling tripod
The castored base enables the mounting to be moved around freely. But its height is fixed.

The pedestal
A highly mobile mounting, with a readily adjustable height. The most widely used mounting in TV studio production.

19

Lens Angles – Themes and Variations

The camera lens fills the screen with a wedge-shaped segment of the scene before it. The actual coverage of this *field of view* may be anything from a very narrow horizontal angle (eg: $1\frac{1}{2}°$) to the extreme wide angle of the 360° 'fish-eye' lens. The normal range used in a TV studio covers around 5° to 50°.

Camera lenses can be designated either in terms of their *focal length* (an optical property), or their *horizontal coverage angles.* The latter have more direct practical value to the director.

Choosing the lens angle

Two forms of camera lens are in use: the *fixed-angle* lens and the *zoom* lens. A careful selection of fixed-angle lenses on a turret camera (eg: 9°, 17°, 27°, 35°) provides useful variation of shot from a given position. The more complex zoom lens system, however, can be adjusted to any angle within its range.

As the TV screen has 4 by 3 proportions, the lens' *vertical* angle of view is 3/4 of its horizontal angle. The *horizontal* angle shows us the exact shot coverage on scale studio plans, and so is invaluable for production planning.

Theoretically our TV viewer will only see *natural perspective* when his eye subtends a similar angle to his TV screen as the TV camera lens. In practice though, a camera lens angle of about 20°–27° produces natural-looking results. However, if we use an appreciably narrower or wider lens angle, pictorial perspective becomes distorted, so that relative sizes, depths, and distances appear different from those in the scene.

We have, therefore, to choose our camera lens-angles carefully, to avoid such accidental *perspective distortion* as a room appearing large in one shot and cramped in another. Paradoxically, we can actually turn this phenomenon to our advantage, to deliberately create visual effects, or overcome problems in production.

Image size and distortion

Our lens fills the TV screen with the scene visible within its angle of view – whether that angle be a few degrees, or a wide coverage. While a narrow-angle lens may see only a single head, a wide-angle shows an entire row of people (we see more, but the size of each part is proportionally reduced). A 10° lens shows a subject 5 times as large as we would see on switching to a 50° lens, but reveals only 1/5 of the scene that a 50° lens would take in. Turn to a 5° lens, and the image would now be twice as large as the 10°, i.e. 10 times the 50° shot.

20

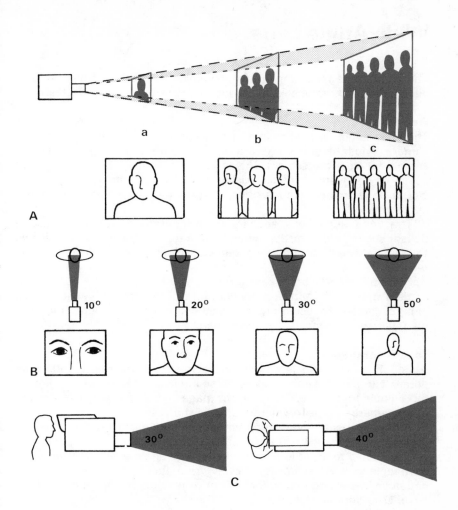

CAMERA LENS ANGLE

(A) Coverage alters with distance
The camera lens shows a rectangular wedge of the scene before it. It therefore covers a larger area at greater distances, than for closer subjects. The closer the subject to the camera, more of the screen it fills. As its distance increases, the subject appears proportionately smaller.

(B) Coverage alters with the lens angle
Changing to a wider lens angle takes in proportionately more of the scene, but the subject image size becomes smaller.

(C) Vertical and horizontal angles
Due to the 4 × 3 picture shape of the TV screen (format, aspect ratio) the vertical angle of the lens is $\frac{3}{4}$ of its horizontal angle.

21

Makes for easier camerawork, but has its limitations, too.

Wide Angle Lens

The *wide angle lens* ranging, for example, from 30–60° has both its advantages and drawbacks in production. Here we list its main features.

Advantages
The wide angle lens takes in a large segment of the scene before the camera. Wider, overall views are obtained without having to move the camera far from the subject. This is a particular advantage in restricted space or congested studios. (Using a normal lens angle, the camera would have to be much further away to get the same shot – often impracticable).

The wide angle lens appears to exaggerate perspective, making distant subjects look further away than in reality. This effect enables us to make a small setting seem quite spacious, even impressively extensive.

Smooth camerawork is easier when using a wide angle lens because camera movement and uneven floors are less liable to cause picture jump or judder. Focusing too is generally less critical (greater depth of field than with normal lens angles – page 23).

Disadvantages
Although wide angle lenses show so much of the scene, individual details can become too small to be seen clearly. Moreover, the lens is more liable to *shoot-off* past the set (page 34), suffer *lens flares,* or get other cameras, lights, or microphones in shot.

Although it can cover action within confined surroundings, the wide angle lens' propensity to exaggerate distance, depth and space, can cause a small room to look unnaturally large or extensive. Furthermore, as people move towards and away from the camera, the speed of action seems exaggerated; they seem to take surprisingly little time to cover considerable distances.

Unless you want grotesquely distorted portraits, avoid close shots of people with wide angle lenses. A screen-filling shot of a head appears quite unflattering – even bizarre.

Wide angle lenses can produce geometrical distortion too; particularly noticeable on shots of music, lines of lettering. So don't pan around on lenses of about 50° or more, if you want to avoid seeing straight verticals curve, and straighten as they pass across the shot.

All these characteristics become more pronounced as the lens angle widens. So, while noticeable at around 35°, they are very evident at 60°, and extremely obvious at wider angles. The *fish-eye* lens, which has a 360° angle of view, provides such distortion that it can only really be used for special effects shots.

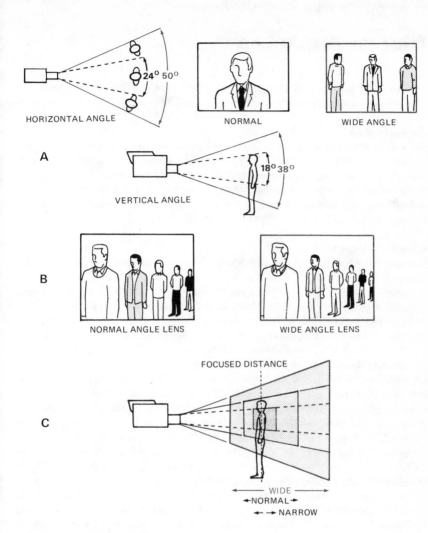

HORIZONTAL ANGLE 24° 50°

NORMAL

WIDE ANGLE

A

VERTICAL ANGLE 18° 38°

B

NORMAL ANGLE LENS

WIDE ANGLE LENS

C

FOCUSED DISTANCE

WIDE
NORMAL
NARROW

USING WIDE ANGLE LENSES

(A) Wide-angle lens
For a given camera position, the wide-angle lens gives an apparently more distant view, and a smaller image of the subject.

(B) The impression of space
Whereas a normal lens-angle (e.g. 24°) provides natural perspective, the wide-angle lens shows apparently exaggerated perspective. (Camera distance adjusted here for same size foreground subject.)

(C) Depth of field
Sharpest at the focused distance, the picture remains substantially sharp over a range of distances nearer and further away. This *depth of field* becomes deeper for wider lens angles (and as focused distance increases; and for smaller lens-stops).

23

Narrow Angle Lens

The *narrow angle* lens (15–5°) provides its own particular production opportunities and problems.

Advantages

As it fills the screen with a restricted area of the scene in front of the camera, the narrow angle lens gives us a 'telescopic' view of the subject. So you can obtain close shots from a distant camera position. This is particularly useful when for some reason (obstacles, uneven ground, insufficient time) you cannot move your camera sufficiently near to the subject to achieve a large image on a normal lens angle.

Disadvantages

Narrow-angle lenses can produce strangely distorted views of the three-dimensional world. Perspective in a distant scene shot with a narrow-angle lens, appears to be *compressed.* Depth looks squashed. Distant subjects seem disproportionately nearer and larger than in the actual scene. *Portraits can look unpleasantly flattened and misshapen,* particularly for three-quarter face and full-face views. Surface modelling (contouring) too, is less evident.

The narrow-angle lens gives the cameraman particular problems. His camera becomes more difficult to handle smoothly, as even a slight amount of shake results in a distractingly exaggerated picture judder. Any movement of the camera mounting is liable to appear uneven and jerky. On *remotes* (OBs) cameras frequently need to use very narrow lens angles (eg: $\frac{1}{2}°$ to 5°) to obtain large enough images of distant, often inaccessible subjects. These problems can therefore become acute. The camera may have to be held rigidly, *locked off* on its panning head, rather than left free, ready to tilt and pan.

The effective depth of field of any narrow angle lens is relatively shallow. Consequently, focusing becomes that much more critical. As you focus the lens on subjects closer to the camera, this shallow depth decreases even further – an embarrassment in close-ups of smaller subjects (page 32). For an audience, a picture with such shallow focused depth can be very trying to watch, because only a part of the subject can be seen clearly, the rest being a defocused blur.

When using very narrow lens angles on location in hot weather, we are liable to find the picture shimmering overall, as a result of heat haze. As this effect results from diffraction produced by hot air currents, the only remedy is to position the camera closer to the subject, using a lens with a slightly wider angle of view.

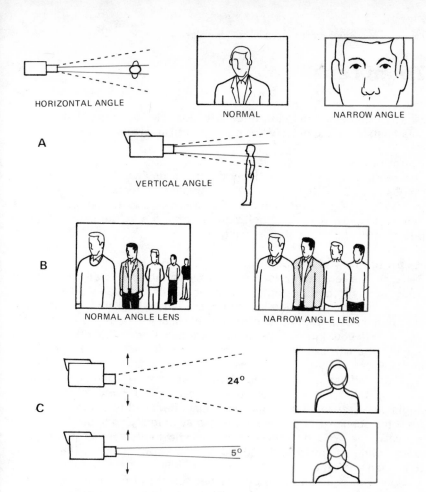

HORIZONTAL ANGLE

NORMAL

NARROW ANGLE

A

VERTICAL ANGLE

B

NORMAL ANGLE LENS

NARROW ANGLE LENS

C

24°

5°

USING NARROW ANGLE LENSES

(A) Narrow-angle lens
For a given camera position, the narrow-angle lens gives an apparently closer view, and a larger image of the subject.

(B) The impression of space
Whereas a normal lens-angle (e.g. 24°) provides a natural perspective, the narrow-angle lens shows apparently compressed perspective. (Camera distance adjusted here, for same size foreground subject.)

(C) Camera handling
Using a 24° lens angle a slight vertical judder of 1° (uneven floor, strong wind) produces a just acceptable jump of $\frac{1}{24}$ picture height. On a 5° lens, the same judder results in a considerable picture jump ($\frac{1}{5}$ of picture height!) With a 50° lens, it varies only $\frac{1}{50}$, and might be overlooked altogether.

25

Zoom Lens

Most TV cameras are being fitted with zoom lenses, for a system with an adjustable angle of view has many practical advantages.

Zoom range

The range of a zoom lens depends on its design. The magnification ranges from 3 : 1 (eg: 10° to 30°) on smaller cameras, to the 10 : 1 (5° to 50°) and 20 : 1 lens systems. (Sometimes an extra, *extender* lens is needed to allow the full range). Where a *shot box* is fitted, there is rapid push-button selection of preset angles.

Its problems and opportunities

Because the lens angle is continuously variable, it is all too easy to select an inappropriate angle, or to alter it indiscriminately. At any given setting (narrow, normal, wide) the zoom lens will exhibit the handling characteristics and distortion of that particular lens angle (pages 22, 24). So if you intercut pictures from cameras using different lens angles, you can expect to get different impressions of distance, depth and proportions.

If you adjust the lens angle while on shot, the familiar effect of *zooming* takes place. Narrow the angle and you *zoom in*. Widen the angle, and you *zoom out*. The superficial effect is that of moving to and from the scene – but you are actually only magnifying and reducing *the same image.* You do not see the realistic movement of planes that arises when you move within the three-dimensional world. The effect is to squash and expand space quite unnaturally.

However, you can zoom on any *flat* subject (a map) to show detail and an overall view, without problems (although camera handling changes with lens angle). In fact, you can usually get smoother, more accurate treatment by zooming to and from the graphics than by moving the camera itself.

Turret lenses confine you to certain lens angles, and if you want a shot slightly tighter or looser than you have, either the subject or the camera mounting has to be moved. The zoom lens, on the other hand, enables you to adjust to any required angle, to trim the shot exactly.

The zoom lens does present one particularly embarrassing hazard for the cameraman. That is, the way in which the available depth of field becomes proportionally shallower, and therefore focus more critical as the lens angle narrows (zooming in). On a wide angle shot, focus adjustment is broad, for there is considerable focused depth. But when zooming in quickly to detail, the narrow angle and diminished depth of field may cause inaccurate close focusing. The only remedy is to *pre-check any zoom-in.* (Zoom in, focus, zoom out to the opening position). This ensures that focus will be sharp when subsequently zooming on shot.

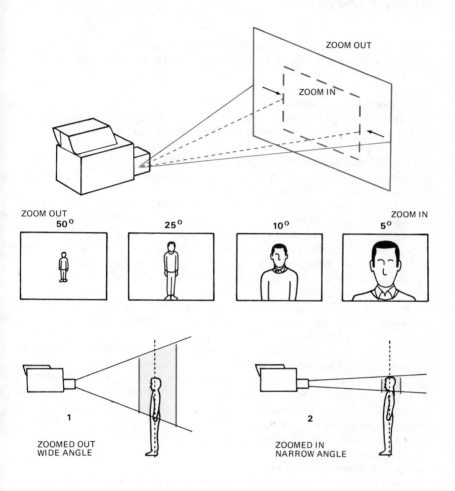

ZOOM OUT

ZOOM IN

ZOOM OUT
50°   25°   10°   ZOOM IN
5°

1
ZOOMED OUT
WIDE ANGLE

2
ZOOMED IN
NARROW ANGLE

ZOOM LENS

Changing the zoom lens-angle
As the lens angle is reduced, and the picture *zooms in,* the image size increases and the area covered decreases proportionally.

Changing characteristics
1. At its widest angle, the zoom lens handles smoothly, and has an increased depth of field.   2. Zoomed in to its narrowest angle, these characteristics reverse, so that camera handling becomes very sensitive, and depth of field quite shallow.

27

Why Zoom?

Properly used, the zoom lens offers flexibility and freedom that would otherwise be unattainable, but used unthinkingly, it can lead to sadly slipshod techniques.

How the zoom can help
The zoom lens has various productional advantages. It is particularly useful where a camera is immobile, or a pedestal is too heavy for free movement, or where the cameraman is inexperienced in handling dollies. Zooming can often be done more rapidly and smoothly than dolly movement. Where only one camera is used, zoom action can increase the variety of shots available.

Unlike the turret camera, the zoom lens-angle can be continuously, silently, changed in a moment, so there is less likelihood of your switching to a camera during a lens change.

You can often disguise the unavoidable effects of perspective distortion during zooming (ie: spatial squashing or stretching) by deliberately doing it *during* camera and/or subject movement, while the audience is distracted.

By slightly adjusting the lens-angle, you can often improve framing, without having to move the camera mounting. This can prove particularly useful when a performer fails to 'hit his marks' (page 119).

If you cut from an overall view of a scene, to a close shot of a small part of it, the audience can become confused or disorientated. In general, therefore, this technique is best avoided. However, where this transition is artistically desirable, to make a particular point, you can zoom in a continuous action from wide to close viewpoints, as an effective visual bridge, without the physical difficulties and time delay that a long *dolly shot (tracking shot)* can involve.

Dramatic use of the zoom
Zoom with care! Zooming must always be a smooth, deliberate effect. Avoid the nauseous results of jerky or 'in and out' zooming. Zooming in to detail enables you to direct attention, to increase tension, to restrict viewpoint, or to give a point powerful emphasis. A *crash zoom-in* hurls detail at the audience. Distance and depth squash dramatically. Conversely, a rapid zoom out creates an illusion of expansion. But obviously these are techniques that can all too easily be over-used. Even more bizarre effects are possible, such as the spatial contortions you see when dollying-in and zooming-out simultaneously.

Such effects should be reserved for those special occasions when they will add an extra value to the treatment. For the most part, the zoom lens should be used at a *normal* viewing angle (around 24°); its wider and narrower angles being used for specific purposes, not as an adjunct to sloppy production routines.

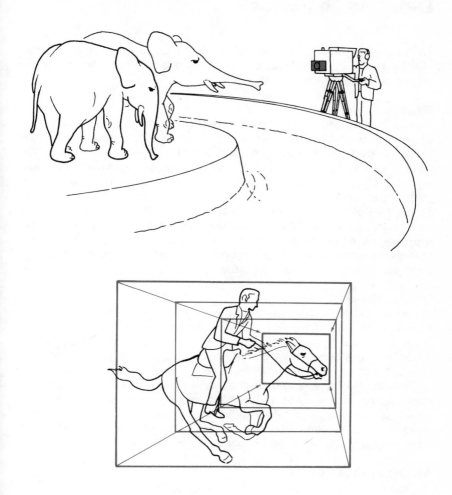

HOW THE ZOOM HELPS

The inaccessible subject
Where the camera cannot reach the subject, the zoom lens enables us to get a variety of shots from a fixed viewpoint.

Disguising the zoom
When the subject is moving rapidly, the camera can zoom over a wide range without the resultant changes being so obvious.

Defining the Shot

To convey the director's ideas quickly and precisely, a system of 'shot classifications' has evolved. Some terms are misused, or imprecise, others vary between organisations.

General terms
Generally speaking, when we classify the *length of shot,* we are considering how much of the screen is being filled by our subject, how close it appears to be, how general or specific a view we have of it. We have the loose terms *long shot* or *full shot* (ie: distant view) and *close shot* or *tight shot* (ie: near view), and *wide shot (cover shot)* to indicate that the camera should take in all the action in a broad view. The camera height, too, is often described in general terms: *top shot* (overhead), *high shot* (steeply inclined downwards), *level shot* (along the eye-line or chest level), *low* or *depressed shot* (upward angled), *low-level shot* (along the floor). In shooting people, we have the approximations: single, 2-shot, 3-shot, group shot.

Getting the shot
When we define a shot, we are indicating the *effect* we want; but not how it is actually achieved. We can, for example, obtain a 'close' or 'tight' shot equally well on a close wide angle lens, or a distant narrow angle lens. The perspective, distortion, camera-handling is different, but the shot-size and the *depth of field* obtained is similar.

We can alter the length of shot by moving the subject and/or the camera, or zooming, or by switching to another camera with a different lens-angle or distance. The audience impact is different for each method. Only movement of the subject or camera actually maintains constant perspective and proportion in the picture.

Choice of shot
TV has developed a reputation for being a 'close-up' medium. But the proportion of close shots should not be overdone. Although the TV screen is, admittedly, too small to do justice to panoramic shots of the 'wide open spaces', or to spectaculars, its restricted size is not unduly inhibiting in practice. As televised motion pictures reveal, medium and long (full) shots effectively reveal a location, establish a mood, or follow action. Only in sustained long shots of detailed scenes (eg: an art gallery) is the viewer likely to find the small detail of the distant view frustrating.

In practice, the type of shots that predominate varies with the kind of production. While a dance assembly usually requires longer shots, a demonstration makes extensive use of close-ups. A dramatic play may equally well explore atmospheric, environmental long shots, and close shots of people and their reactions, according to the plot situation.

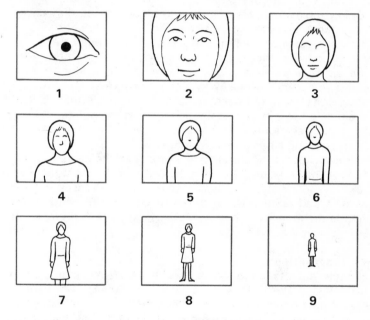

BASIC SHOTS

Shot classification

Although nomenclature varies between countries and even studios, these basic shots are widely used:

1. Extreme Close-up (ECU, detail shot): Isolated detail.
2. Face shot (VCU, very close-up): Head cut at mid-forehead, and above chin.
3. Big close-up (BCU, tight close-up, large head, full head): Full head-height fills screen.
4. Close-up (CU, head and shoulders): framed a short distance above head, down to upper chest.
5. Medium Close-up (MCU, bust shot, chest shot): Cuts body at lower chest.
6. Mid-shot (MS, waist shot, close medium shot): Cuts body at waist.
7. Three-quarter Shot (medium shot, knee shot): Cuts body around knees.
8. Full-length Shot (FLS, MLS, medium long shot): takes in entire body, plus a short distance above and below it.
9. Long Shot (LS): Person occupies $\frac{1}{3}$ to $\frac{3}{4}$ screen height.

Requiring care from the cameraman and performer alike.

Close Shots

Close shots can show details of large objects, or provide magnified views of smaller ones. But they bring their headaches, and it is as well for the director to appreciate their limitations.

Cameraman's problems

As the camera gets closer, the available depth of field diminishes (page 23). So it may not be possible to hold the subject in sharp focus overall. Instead, you can only focus on the most important plane, leaving the rest unsharp. (You can overcome this problem by taking a longer shot, or stopping the lens down, but each remedy has its drawbacks.) To focus as sharply as possible on small items, they should be held quite still, preferably resting on a firm surface at a prearranged mark.

Cameras cannot focus on subjects closer than their *minimum focusing distance* indicates. This varies with lens design, from a few millimetres to several metres away. Even where close focusing is possible, though, the depth of field may be embarrassingly shallow. Lighting can be difficult, too – in getting enough light, at the right angle, without casting camera shadows onto the subject. So you often have to work further away, using a narrower lens angle.

The closer the shot, the greater the problems the cameraman has in accommodating or following action. To and fro movement requires very precise focus-following, and lateral action easily passes outside the framed area and is lost. The results can be quite frustrating! Equally annoying is the inability to discern detail, or to read information due to unsharp pictures (page 134).

Production problems

Although close shots reveal detail, this should be relevant, appropriate and interesting. Detail may look crude, or reveal blemishes. The audience should *want to see* this close view (or be persuaded to want it), not feel prevented from seeing other aspects that seem more interesting to them.

Close shots preclude the audience from seeing the overall view. If you use them to excess, therefore, you can prevent people from getting a clear idea of spatial relationships, or realising where things are in the scene. They can lose a concept of proportion and scale. By moving in to very close shots, however, you can often help the viewer to appreciate craftsmanship, and subtleties that he would otherwise overlook in longer shots. Screen-filling shots of people may appear dramatic. But they can equally well emphasise complexion or dental defects.

Very close cameras can distract performers and prevent other cameras from seeing the subject. Consequently, you often find yourself taking close-ups from a distance with a narrow lens angle, notwithstanding perspective and handling disadvantages.

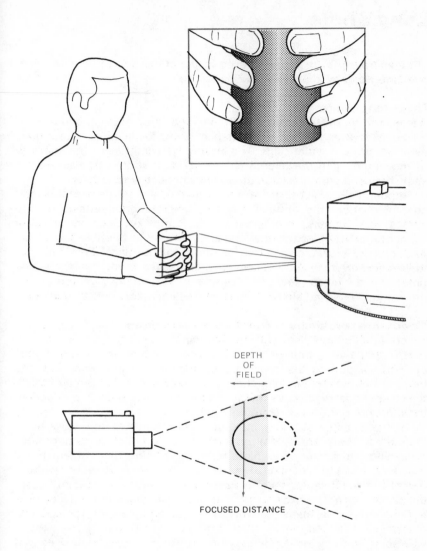

DEPTH
OF
FIELD

FOCUSED DISTANCE

CLOSE SHOTS

Action area
The action area in very close shots becomes extremely limited, and movements easily pass outside the shot. It is best to rest the item on a firm surface, at a marked position.

Depth of field
In close shots, the depth of field can become so restricted, that only part of the subject is sharply focused, the rest becoming an indistinct blur.

33

Long Shots

The general term *long shot* is used in the studio for any area of view over about 3·5 by 2·5 metres (12 by 9 feet).

Using long shots

Because *long shots* give a broad coverage, they allow the viewer to follow widespread action – of a dance team, for instance – and helps establish group relationships. Too close a viewpoint loses the interplay of movement, and the overall pattern. Distant shots can also help to show how one part or section of a scene connects with others.

Although closer shots are necessary to reveal performer reaction and characterisation, the atmospheric and environmental effects due to staging and lighting are largely lost. Some TV directors make a deliberate point of including a long shot as soon as possible in a scene, to show the viewer where the action is taking place. From this *establishing shot,* they cut to closer viewpoints. Too often, that is the only time the audience sees the complete setting! A well-presented production, however, aims at a balanced selection of shots throughout.

Operational problems in continuous production

A very practical problem with the long shot is that it easily shows *too much!* You may shoot off past the edges of the set, seeing lights, perhaps, or getting the sound boom and other cameras in shot. As focus is sharp overall in long shots (due to considerable depth of field), these spurious details are quite visible. In a continuous production, therefore, long shots need forethought.

To avoid cameras coming into shot when changing from close-up to long shots, there are several options. You can dolly the camera back from close to distant viewpoints (time consuming; the camera move may be irrelevant). You can zoom out (the magnification alters without natural perspective changes). You can cut from a fairly distant 'close-up' camera using a narrow angle lens, to a wide angle lens on a camera a similar distance away, covering a larger area (despite perspective differences). Or you can position the close-up camera at an oblique viewpoint, even hiding it behind scenery to keep it out of view. Finally, if all else fails, you may have to resort to the trickery of *edited-in* close-ups, or *cutaways* to photographs of the details that you want to show in close shots. Whichever of these expedients is used, it should be *artistically appropriate*; for each has its particular limitations.

When pulling out to a long shot (by dollying or zooming), ensure that the widening view does not inadvertently reveal other cameras or shoot off. It may be necessary to clear (pull back) other cameras to prevent this happening.

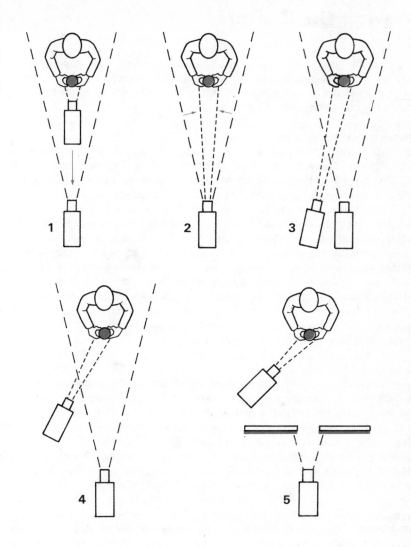

AVOIDING CAMERAS IN SHOT

Transitions from close to distant viewpoints

To avoid another camera appearing in picture when changing from close-up to a longer shot various methods are used: 1. Trucking (tracking) the camera out. 2. Zooming out.   3. Cutting between nearly equidistant cameras (similar viewpoints) with different lens angles.   4. Obliquely-angled close-up camera (out of shot, but closer).   5. Hidden close-up camera.

Moving the Camera

The mobility of a camera, depends upon the type and design of its mounting. The wise director therefore takes into account exactly what his cameras can do, and how smoothly they can do it, when planning production treatment.

Camera moves
Apart from trying to ensure that the more complex shots fall to the most experienced cameramen, the director rightly leaves the actual operational difficulties to his crew. However, it is as well to be aware of typical problems, for these directly affect techniques.

If a camera pedestal is heavy, the inertia when it is started or stopped, is considerable, and prevents smooth rapid repositioning. It is easier to push in or pull out a pedestal (particularly along a straight line), than to *arc* round a subject in a curved track, or to move across the scene *(truck, crab, chinese)*. On most pedestals, too, it takes a moment to change the wheel mechanism from steering in a *dollying (tracking)* mode, to the *trucking (crabbing)* mode for transverse moves.

Remember that when you use narrow lens angles to keep cameras back out of shot, all their movements look proportionally coarser, less steady, and liable to bounce or weave.

Focusing
A cameraman normally maintains sharp focus on the principal subject. He *follows focus* as the subject-to-camera distance varies. How critical focusing is, depends on this distance, the lens angle used (its depth of field) and the amount of subject detail. Close shots of very fine detail using narrow lens angles are most exacting.

Where the relative distances of subjects differ too much for the camera to focus sharply overall, there are several remedies. You can focus *hard* on one of them, allowing others to remain in *soft focus*. You can *split focus* so that the farthest and nearest are equally focused (although neither will be really sharp). You can move the subjects to make them more equidistant from the camera. Finally, you can stop the lens down (reduce its aperture) to increase the depth of field. But this necessitates greatly increased light levels overall, to compensate exposure.

When both the subject and camera are moving, focus following is essential. In such *running shots,* the cameraman must continually anticipate the amount of focused depth available, to maintain sharp focus. Where the camera is moving to or from a flat surface – a map, chart, music or book – he continually 'creeps' the focus to maintain optimum sharpness; an operation that can require considerable skill. The alternative operation is to zoom, but that too has its focusing dilemmas (page 26).

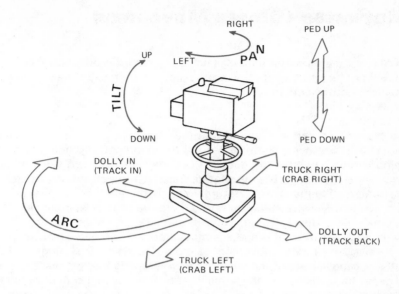

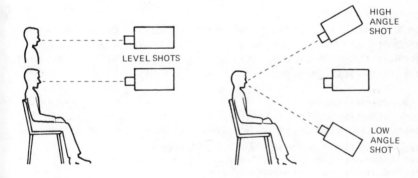

ADJUSTING THE CAMERA

Camera moves

The camera can be moved around and repositioned in various ways. As this diagram shows, the Pedestal offers considerable mobility.

Camera height

The camera is *level* to a person at around chin height. The mounting should be higher for a standing position, than for a seated one. High-angle shots, and low-angle shots can be obtained by adjusting the camera height, by positioning the subject, or by mirrors.

37

Motivated Camera Movement

Ideally, all camerawork should have a *motivated* production value. It should not just create visual variety, relieve monotony, or help to make way for another camera.

Motivation

If a move has no artistic purpose, it draws attention to itself as intrusive mechanics. A move may be a natural development; eg: going in as a demonstrator points to details. Or we can deliberately *create motivation*. Someone who is seated, gets up to fetch a book to show the camera. The move looks natural enough, but enables the director to activate an otherwise static shot. When we need to adjust mechanics to suit new shot development, we can similarly create motivation. The move looks natural, but is actually motivated by *contrived business.*

Excessive camera movement appears restless, and fidgety. Insufficient movement of the subject or camera, and interest wanes. Too frequent movement, and the value of each move is reduced. But during a static scene, even a single well-conceived movement can have a dramatic impact.

Panning

Panning should be a smooth, deliberate, continuous operation. Do not pan over a wide arc just to relocate the shot, eg: between guests in an interview. Cut between them instead. Use fast pans *(whip, zip* or *swish* pan) only for startling effect.

Viewpoint changes

Static, shoulder-level shots form the core of TV studio presentation. But we often want to change this viewpoint. Let us consider *why* we move.

Moving in to the subject (dolly or track in, zoom in). We move in to see more detail; to concentrate attention; to exclude extraneous subjects; to identify detail; to alter scale; to follow a subject as it moves away.

Moving out from the subject (dolly or track back; zoom out). We move out to accommodate wider action; to show a subject's relationship to its surroundings; to take in more subjects; to reveal the reason for a person's move; to follow someone moving away from the camera; to broaden information (from a solo singer to an entire choir); as an act of conclusion to action.

Moving across the scene (truck, crab). Here we follow transverse subject movement; or survey a broad, long, spread-out subject; or a succession of subjects.

Moving round the subject (arcing). Moving round a subject we can alter our scenic viewpoint; show different aspects of the subject and its surroundings; create visual variety; change the centre of interest; or recompose the shot to alter emphasis.

Moving to a higher viewpoint (ped up, elevate, boom or crane up). High angle shots can provide overall views; enable us to see over obstacles; or obtain level shots of tall or elevated subjects.

Lower camera viewpoints (ped down, depress, boom or crane down). Very low positions give dramatic upward-looking shots, while low level shots (ground shots, floor shots) give head-on views of ground level subjects.

38

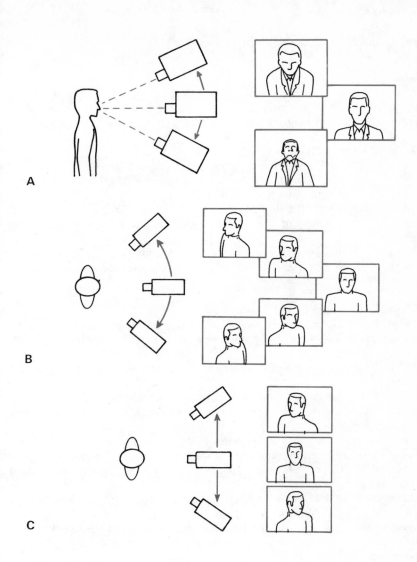

CAMERA VIEWPOINT

(A) Camera height
When the camera looks down, the subject tends to appear inferior, subdued.
Looking upwards, it seems dominant, powerful.

(B) Arcing movement
As the camera moves *round,* a subject can appear to turn.

(C) Trucking (crabbing) movement
As the camera moves *across* the scene, it obtains a more oblique view of the
subject.

Composing the Picture

In 'composing' a picture, we are deliberately framing and positioning subjects to create an artistically appropriate effect. We aim to direct attention, and to develop a particular audience reaction.

General approaches
Flat subjects (paintings, maps) should be shot straight-on to avoid distortion. But solid objects and scenes in depth are often best shot more obliquely, slightly angled to the lens axis.

Avoid haphazard distribution of items in a picture, or confused bunching, or strung-out displays. Instead, aim to form related, unified groups.

Foreground items (people, scenery) can emphasise or enhance the illusion of depth. But avoid continual peering through foreground tracery, foliage, fences, etc.

Arranging people
People need to stand or sit surprisingly close together to look natural on screen. Avoid large central gaps between them. If necessary, take oblique, *cross shots.*

Do not line people up across the shot, but vary their distances from the camera.

Avoid people masking each other, cutting off parts of faces.

Have movement to and from camera, or diagonally, rather than across the screen.

Avoid entrances or exits through the sides of the frame.

Avoid close shots combining both standing *and* seated persons.

Offset all shots of profiles, or 3/4-shots of people. Such *looking room* improves picture balance.

Avoid such accidental effects as scenery, props, etc., behind people, becoming 'halos', 'wings', 'horns', 'hats'.

Avoid lines in the scene cutting across people (eg: at shoulders, knees).

Framing
Keep important items in the shot away from the picture edges.

Headroom should suit the length of shot, and be similar in comparable shots.

Avoid excess space around subjects, or overcrowding in the shot.

Do not let subjects lean or rest on the frame.

Angle shots
Avoid taking all shots from a level position, but alter camera height only for a deliberate purpose. Camera height can affect picture impact. Low angle shots dramatise situations and people. High shots reduce their impact and importance.

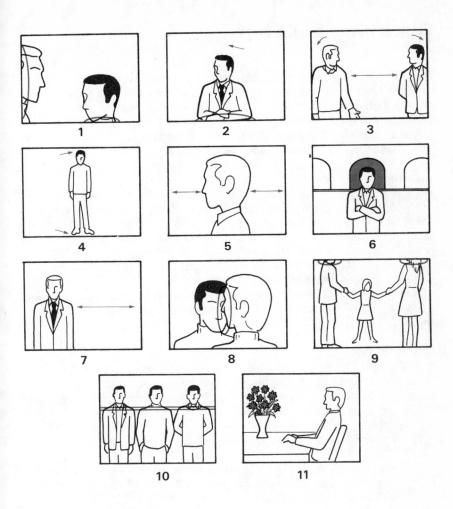

COMPOSING THE PICTURE

Shots to avoid

Here are various everyday compositional errors you should avoid.
1. Avoid half-heads, and body-less shots.   2. Avoid excess headroom. People should not rest on the frame.   3. Avoid excess empty space between subjects. Do not have subjects too near the sides of the shot.   4. This shot is too tightly framed, with too little space at the top and bottom.   5. Always offset a profile of $\frac{3}{4}$-face shot, to give it 'looking room'.   6. Avoid lines cutting a person, or adding spurious extensions.   7. Centralise subjects unless they are balanced by scenic masses.   8. Avoid foreground subjects masking others.   9. Avoid decapitation.   10. Don't align subjects across the screen (vary size, distance, and position).   11. Avoid over-prominent set-dressing (props).

Clarifying the Shot

Directly a shot appears on the screen, the viewer's eyes scan the picture for information. He assesses, interprets and relates the new shot to the previous one. If the viewer cannot see the subject clearly, or looks at the wrong aspect of the shot, he is diverted and wrong ideas develop. How subjects are displayed therefore, has an important influence on how effectively ideas are conveyed to the audience.

Improving clarity
Do not try to show too much at a time. Simplify grouping, and avoid over-complex arrangements, or dual centres of attention. However, if presentation is continually stark and basic (objects isolated against plain backgrounds), the results can be pictorially dull. Over-elaborate crowded shots, on the other hand, are liable to distract the viewer's attention. Background tones should be subdued, but contrast with the subject, without fussy detail.

Clarity can depend on the camera viewpoint. Even common objects become puzzle pictures if shot from inappropriate angles. Try to avoid important parts of subjects becoming obscured or shadowed.

Clarity of detail
Visual clarity can be lost in shots that are too close or too distant from the subject. Detail is hard to discern in a small image. But in too close a shot, this detail can become unrecognisably over-enlarged. Over-close shots of photographs, engravings, book illustrations, can actually reduce their clarity. The viewer cannot gain extra information but instead sees fuzzy detailless shadows, or evidence of dot or line structure.

The way in which restricted focused depth prevents one from seeing subjects clearly was discussed on pages 23, 27, 33. But we can turn this phenomenon to our advantage. By making distant (and nearer) subjects an indistinguishable blur, we can visually isolate the subject. Soft focusing can be disturbing, though, where objects can neither be seen clearly, nor ignored altogether. Defocused foreground items can prove very intrusive (eg: an unsharp vase of flowers).

Ironically, if everything in a shot is needle-sharp (deep focus), clarity can be impaired, as planes at quite different distances from the camera appear to merge in the flat TV picture. Only variations in brightness, colour, or form help us to decipher the scene.

Lighting can enhance or obscure clarity – accidentally or deliberately. Shadow or reflections can prevent our seeing details. Diffuse *(soft)* light can suppress texture and surface modelling. Lit from an unsuitable angle, the shape or details of an object can be lost or reduced.

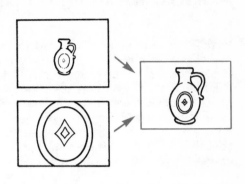

Size of shot
If the shot is too distant, details cannot be seen. Too close, and details are coarsened, and the outline lost.

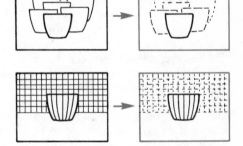

Conflicting backgrounds
Congested or over-detailed backgrounds can be supressed by deliberately limiting the depth of field.

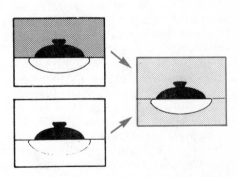

Background tones
Background tones should be arranged to suit the subject – whether by lighting adjustment, or choice of surface values.

43

Video Switching – Vision Mixing

Each TV picture source is routed to the *video switching panel (video switcher, vision mixer)* in the production control room. Where the show is straightforward, or camera mobility limited (as in most remotes or OBs), and where spontaneous shot selection is essential, the director himself can switch successfully. But where he is very preoccupied with production operations (guiding camera moves and composition, cueing, etc.) and complex switching operations develop, it is better for a specialist *(switcher, vision mixer)* or the *technical director* (page 15) to operate the panel instead.

Basic operation

The equipment itself is fundamentally simple to operate. The skill lies in selecting the right sources at exactly the right moment, using the appropriate transition. In a fast, complicated show, this is no mean feat, particularly where several video sources are combined. Two fundamental console designs are widely used, one with a video fader for each source, and another, using a communal pair of fading levers.

Let us look first at the more flexible, and more expensive 'fader per channel' design. Pushing the appropriate source button, switches its picture immediately on to the *main channel (transmission, studio output).* Pushing another, cuts instantly to *that* picture instead.

Above each *cut* or *take button* is the *fader* for that channel. By pushing the fader upwards this picture gradually becomes visible *(fading up, fading in)* from black to full brightness. Moving it downwards gives a *fade out (fade down)* to black. When two (or more) sources are faded up, we transparently *superimpose (super)* their shots. We can fade out one source from a dual superimposition *(take it out),* to leave a single picture. Simultaneously fading up one picture while fading out another, *mixes (dissolves, cross-fades)* as they blend temporarily.

More complex video switching panels have dual construction, consisting of two identical *banks (buses).* This enables us to set up a chosen balanced selection of sources on the second bank *('B' bank, effects bank, mix-bank)* while the *main bank ('A' bank, program bank)* is principally used for straight switching between individual sources. Master controls enable us to cross-fade, super, or intercut between these pre-set groups, and to obtain picture combinations.

The alternative video-switcher design, using a communal pair of fading levers, is less adaptable, but simple to operate. Operational techniques are shown in the illustration opposite.

The most sophisticated consoles offer a wide range of facilities, including: *wipes, split-screen* (pages 46, 153, 167) *chroma-key* (page 152), *colour synthesizer selection* (page 144), *title-edging* (page 144), as well as monitor switching, remote activation of slide scanner, film channel, videotape, etc.

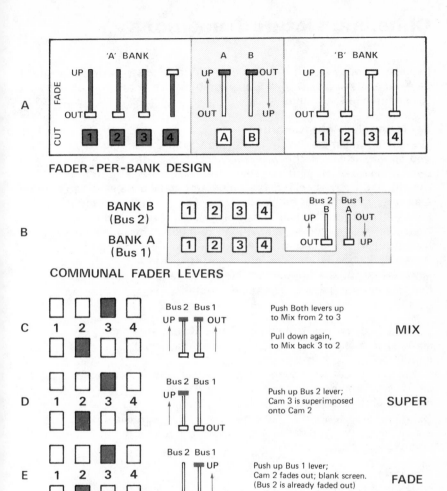

FADER-PER-BANK DESIGN

COMMUNAL FADER LEVERS

VIDEO SWITCHING

(A) Fader per channel design

The central master faders used together, select either bank. Sources on that bank can be switched, or faded up/down. Using master faders individually, the two banks can be blended, or combinations interswitched.

(B) Communal fader levers

Switching here is normally by buttons on the lower row (Bus 1./Bank A). Pushing the fading levers up, the top set of buttons becomes operative instead.
Diagrams show (C) mix, (D) super, and (E) fade operations.

Choosing Picture Transitions

Because in television it is only necessary to press a button or move a fader to achieve any type of transition between shots, it is all too easy to use them indiscriminately.

Selecting the right transition
We should never be casual about a transition. It should be motivated, and appropriate. Whether we *cut, mix* or *wipe,* affects the 'feel' of that part of the production. It can even alter the audience's interpretation of the shots. Strictly speaking, we should not make a transition to another shot until the first has fulfilled its purpose – the information in the first shot is absorbed or its action completed. If a shot is held for too *short* a time, the information or the action are incomplete or disrupted. If we hold it for too *long,* attention wanders. How long we can hold a shot, therefore, depends on how interesting it is, the action it contains, its significance for the production, the mood required, and so on. Wrong use causes ambiguity, confusion, distraction.

The cut
The cut is dynamic. It makes an immediate comparison between two shots. There is continuity. The action of the respective shots appears continuous.

Preferably, cut on movement within the frame – as a person gets up, as a head turns or on an exit. A cut on dialogue (not necessarily at the end of sentences) gives emphasis. But remember, where a cut *interrupts* action (during a movement, or within a musical phrase) it can disrupt its flow. In general, it is advisable not to intercut between still and moving shots.

The fade
Fades in and out of black generally denote a long lapse of time. How long, depends on the fade rate. *Slow fades* have a smooth, gentle, peaceful connotation. The *fade in* is an introductory, opening transition. The *fade out* conveys conclusion or dying away.

The mix (dissolve)
The mix is a comparative transition, drawing attention to similarities or differences between subjects. A mix may imply a short time lapse. *Fast mixes* tend to indicate concurrent, parallel action. *Slow mixes* provide uninterrupted picture flow – quiet, restful transitions. They may suggest transfers in time or space.

Wipes
Wipes are essentially decorative devices. One picture breaks in to another, obliterating it partly or totally. The shape, speed, direction (and edge-hardness) are adjusted to suit the effect required.

PICTURE TRANSITIONS

The cut
An instantaneous change from one picture source to another.

The fade–out
The gradual fade out of a picture, to a black screen. The *fade-up* is the reverse effect.

The mix
A simultaneous fade out of one picture, while fading up another. During the mix, the pictures are superimposed.

The wipe
A moving geometrical shape covers over one picture with the corresponding part of another, progressively replacing it. At a midway point, we have a split-screen effect.

Intercut Shots

To transfer the viewer's attention to another subject, or a fresh aspect, we can often simply pan and zoom from one to another. But 'hosepiping' techniques, in which the camera continually pans across the scene, look indecisive and amateurish. If we do not want to move the camera around (pages 36, 37), it is usually more effective to cut to another viewpoint.

Effect of cutting
Cutting is comparative. Instantly, we relate the two shots – their significance, their subjects, viewpoints, directions, speeds. We can make good productional use of this effect, but have to guard against suggesting such relationships *accidentally.* The results can be quite disturbing – or amusing – as can be seen in the common hazards summarized opposite.

Typical treatment
During any interview, discussion, or talk situation, we usually *cross-cut* between the speakers, watching their delivery and reactions (page 160). Clearly, if these shots are too closely matched, undesirable effects can arise. Instead, a certain amount of variation is preferable although it should not be so diverse as to disrupt the visual flow.

Above all, never cut between *nearly identical* shots of the same subject(s). It is surprising how often, when left to devise their own shots, a team of cameramen can unknowingly present a series of similar pictures. Switching between them may achieve nothing but disconcerting visual jumps.

An allied problem can arise when filming a person in a continuous take. If subsequently any material must be edited out a jump-cut results, due to subject movement. Mixing between sections may 'soften-off' this disruption, but the result is still unattractive. It is preferable to introduce *cutaway shots* or *reaction shots* (nod shots) instead, as on page 158.

Reverse-angle shots, in which a person (or part of him) is included in consecutive frontal and rear viewpoints *(over-shoulder shots),* are regularly used when shooting people or locations. This technique helps the viewer to establish or maintain a clear spatial relationship between the subjects. But, if using this, be careful to ensure that the intercutting cameras are on the same side of the *imaginary line* that joins these subjects (page 81). Otherwise, *reverse cuts* can result, as subjects appear to exchange positions in the frame! Although some directors ignore the problem (through insensitivity or perversity), the spurious disturbance to the viewer, as he searches the picture to see where the static subject has now gone, hardly contributes to the presentation!

Transformations

When we cut between identical shots of different subjects, transformations take place.

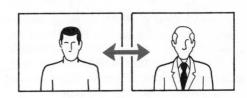

Size jumps

'Shrinkage' or 'growth' occurs on cutting to a different shot size of the subject from a similar angle.

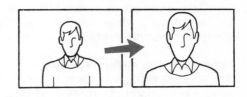

Position twists

Cutting to a similar shot of the subject, from a different angle, can create a visual 'twist'.

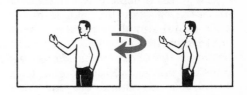

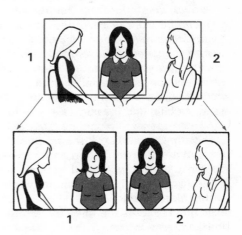

Frame jump (jump cut)

Here the frame position of the subject changes on the cut.

Audio Pick-up Methods

Audio pick-up involves so much more than just being able to *hear* the sound. Its quality should be as realistic as possible, neither dominating nor being swamped by other wanted sounds, its scale should be appropriate to the subject, and to the shot size, and its volume range controlled within the dynamic limits of the audio system.

If such finesse is disregarded, the resultant sound may vary in quality, be sibilant, muffled, distorted or unnatural and accompanied by spurious rustles, crackles or thumps. It may also be of inappropriate scale or proportions, often becoming inaudible or indiscernible. Successful audio pick-up requires carefully selected techniques – in the choice of microphone, placement, and control of audio level.

Approaches to audio pick-up

The simplest pick-up method involves clipping a *personal microphone* on to a person's clothing *(electret* lapel mike or tie-clip), or hanging it round his neck on a cord (*lavalier* mic; *lanyard* mic). These systems are widely used, particularly where more sophisticated facilities or expertise are not available. The mike is either attached to a trailing wire, or plugged into a small personal transmitter.

Static mikes can be used near performers, in the form of *desk (table)* fittings, a *floor-stand,* or a *slung, (hanging)* or static boom mike. But these are not visually acceptable for many presentations. Experienced interviewers, commentators (and singers) may use a *hand-mike* or even a special *lip-mike (noise-cancelling mike).*

To pick up sound from people who are moving around, a personal mike can be used or each person can 'work' to a series of strategically placed static mikes. But unquestionably, optimum audio quality comes only from a carefully positioned movable mike controlled by a specialist operator (audio man, boom man, sound floor operator). The simplest apparatus consists of a mike on the end of a pole (fish-pole; fishing rod), which he directs towards sound sources. Despite its primitive form, it is highly mobile, and invaluable in confined spaces. Alternatively, a small, highly directional microphone *(shot-gun, rifle)* may be used.

The *small (medium) sound boom (small giraffe)* enables one to suspend a mike near action on its pre-set boom arm, and to turn or tilt the mike to follow limited action. But its stretch is restricted (e.g.: 2·1–2·75m, 7–9ft.), and tripod moves are somewhat perilous.

The *large sound boom* (Mole, Fisher) is a much more elaborate facility, that allows the mike to be tilted and turned on its long extendible boom arm, which can swing around and follow subjects from about 2·5–6m (8–20ft.) away. This type of sound boom is used professionally for wide area pick-up of high quality sound. However, it requires skilled operation to achieve this, and to prevent the mike coming into shot, or casting shadows on the performers or the background.

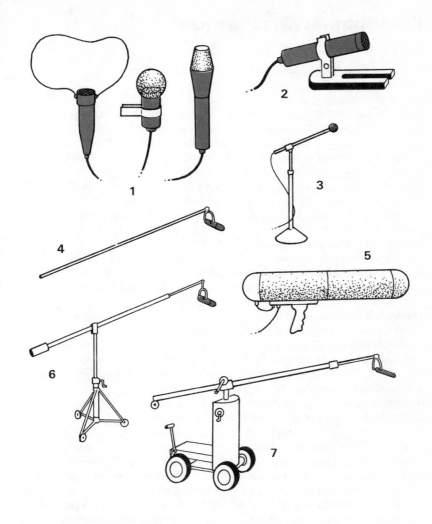

Microphones and stands

1. PERSONAL MIKE. Small microphones round the neck, attached to the clothing, or held by the performer, provide simple audio pick-up.   2. DESK MIKE. A small adjustable stand supports the mike at any angle.   3.STAND MIKE. A lightweight tube or stalk, enabling the mike to be located near a singer or an instrumentalist.   4. FISHPOLE (FISHING ROD). A firm lightweight pole, holding a microphone at its far end. Invaluable for fairly close, but otherwise inaccessible sound pick-up.   5. RIFLE (SHOT GUN) MIKE. Used for pick-up of distant sound over a narrow angle. Able to isolate individual sources within a group.   6. SMALL BOOM. A wheeled tripod supporting the mike at the far end of a pre-adjusted arm. Controls can turn and tilt the mike.   7. SOUND BOOM. Found in larger studios for flexible sound pick-up over a wide area. The arm-length and direction can be changed quickly, and the mike direction and tilt adjusted to follow performers movements.

Anticipation saves valuable rehearsal time.

Planning Audio Pick-up

The wise director does his best to anticipate the unexpected.

Local pick-up
Table mikes or *stand mikes* can be fine for a round-table discussion. But it must always be hoped that the performers will not thump the table, turn away from the mike, rustle papers, or kick the mike stand.

Small *personal mikes* may offer an ideal solution. They are just clipped to the tie, shirt or lapel. But there will always be the performer who taps or scratches his chest, covers the mike, talks to and from it, or is picked up strongly on his neighbour's mike. *Radio mike* systems (a personal mike with a pocket transmitter) appear to give freedom of movement, but are expensive, and can suffer from interference and fading. So they are not an invariable panacea for audio pick-up problems. The alternative is a long trailing connecting lead from the personal mike to a wall socket. Apart from the encumberance of having to drag this around, there is always the risk of getting it entangled.

Using the sound boom
Where more sophisticated, higher quality sound pick-up is required, a *sound boom* mike is essential. Its operator can 'favour' a weak source, and reduce the prominence of a strong one, by carefully angling a directional mike. Similarly, he can reduce unwanted sound reflections from nearby walls, to obtain 'cleaner' sound unmasked by reverberations. He can ensure that people are always clearly on-mike, and not speaking across or away from it.

However, these things are only possible if the boom is skilfully operated and correctly placed for the action. Our basic planning questions are: *Can the boom mike reach the action?* The subject may be too near to the boom or too distant. *Is the boom in the best position to cover the action?* A centre-floor location tends to have best coverage, flanked by cross-shooting cameras. Because the boom necessarily casts shadows (which have to be arranged to fall out of shot) its operation both affects and is affected by, the lighting treatment. *Is there room for the boom to swing?* We must ensure that hanging objects, arches, ceilings, do not entangle or impede boom movement. Or we must allow for sound discontinuity – using one mike to take over from another as the subject moves around. *Is the action widespread?* A boom can accommodate people up to about 2m (6–7ft.) apart. If they are more widely spaced, we may have to move them closer together, favour one source, swing between them during pauses in speech, or use a second mike. The answers are not always evident, and although primarily the sound man's problems, the director may well need to modify subjects' positions, shots, or action to achieve good sound for his production.

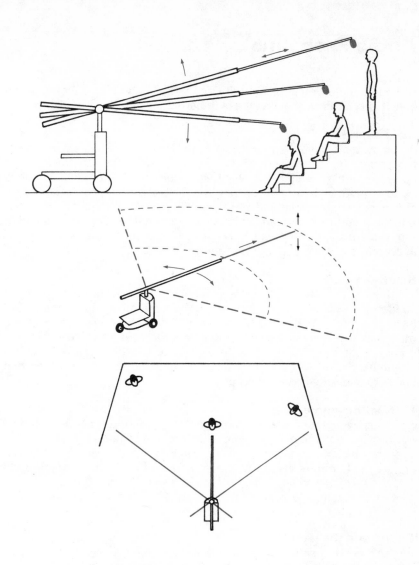

AUDIO PICK-UP

Sound boom coverage

The effective length of the boom arm can be changed, and its angle tilted, to suit variations in the subject distance and height.

The sound boom can swing over a wide arc (360° max.), and tilt vertically over some 20°, enabling it to follow sound within a considerable area.

A central boom position enables it to cover the acting area most efficiently.

Audio Problems

Although audio problems are admittedly the sound man's worry, in the end, it is *your* show that has these imperfections!

Ideal sound
Audio systems have their quirks. They prefer sound sources that are not too *quiet*, for quiet sounds can become lost amidst background noises – ventilation systems, wind, etc. Nor should reproduced sounds be too *loud* for the system or they will distort, and appear out of scale. The audio engineer (sound mixer, audio control man) therefore continually monitors audio amplification, adjusting it to keep sounds within the system's limits *(dynamic range)*, and ensures that they are of appropriate relative strength (the sound balance).

Relative volume
Troubles arise when people speak against loud background noises or sudden loud noises. If they turn away from the mike quickly the sound level and intelligibility may suffer. Audibility may be lost too, where a mike picks up two people speaking with very different voice levels. It is good practice in a talks show to anticipate this dilemma by taking a preliminary *level test,* each participant speaking in turn in his normal voice, to check their voice strengths.

Distracting sound
Spurious background sounds can be quite distracting. Apart from the all too familiar obtrusion of coughs, whispers and footsteps, there are the everyday noises around us that the ear may ignore, but the mike exaggerates. Furniture creaks (wicker chairs and rockers are notorious!), and the rattling and jingling of bracelets and bangles are typical examples. On exterior locations, there may be passing aircraft, traffic, children at play, power-saws, etc., to cope with.

Sound and the picture
Smooth-flowing sound continuity does not come about automatically. We particularly have to ensure that there is homogeneity when a scene is shot out of sequence. An interior must not sound acoustically *dead* in one shot and *live* (reverberant) in another. Background sounds should seem continuous (ie: music, birdsong, traffic, rain, etc.). Such sounds can be added afterwards when editing and dubbing the show, perhaps with *overlays (bridging sounds)* from one scene to the next.

Audio circuitry *(presence filters, equalisation)* can modify sound quality considerably. Reverberation can be added (but never reduced) by suitable devices. Some video switching consoles provide simultaneous video/audio switching, and this facility permits 'clean' intercutting between two scenes, and their associated sound.

AUDIO PROBLEMS

Uneven voice levels
Where quiet voices and loud voices are speaking at the same time the audio
system is left at a disadvantage.

Background noise
Where there is a high level of background noise, speech may become inaudible.

Staging

TV studio scenery generally takes the form of specially-devised, prefabricated, modular or built structures.

Function of staging
Staging (scenic design) does so much more than just provide a background to action. It creates an appropriate environment, giving the production a sense of authority and occasion. Staging can build up an atmosphere or engender a mood. It can re-create a particular location, provide neutral, unassociated surroundings or decorative effects.

Staging can be designed for an individual production, or to provide a utility or semi-permanent background for many. Its complexity may range from painstaking replicas, to a *cyclorama* (a high, stretched cloth backdrop) augmented by built or standing pieces.

Devising scenic treatment
Staging concepts can originate with either the director, or the designer. The director may himself indicate the staging format he requires for his visualisation and treatment of the production, and from that brief, the designer interprets and builds. More often, the scenic designer conceives workable staging arrangements, based on the script and on preliminary talks, and submits this rough plan (perhaps with sketches) for the director's appraisal. The director then devises his shots within this design, including any particularly staged shot opportunities.

Typical design considerations
Staging treatment has to be arranged and organised within very practical parameters if it is to be successful. It must keep within its allocated budget. Its design must be appropriate to the subject, and to the production's purpose. The scenery must be sufficiently ruggedly built to withstand transportation, yet suitable for easy handling. Scenery must be related to studio dimensions and facilities. (It is of little use if it does not go through the supply doors!)

Within the studio, the staging treatment must provide adequate opportunities for performance, and variety of action. It must allow sufficient space for the movement and positioning of cameras, sound booms and lights. Structural safety, fire hazards, and similar factors have to be considered. Its design and structure must permit optimum lighting treatment.

And, of course, the design must suit the director's requirements, providing him with maximum flexibility throughout the production, anticipating as far as possible any potential difficulties.

Scenic design will usually include *set decoration (dressing)*, the furnishing and decorative arrangements *(properties)* for the show and, perhaps, organisation of graphics and/or titling.

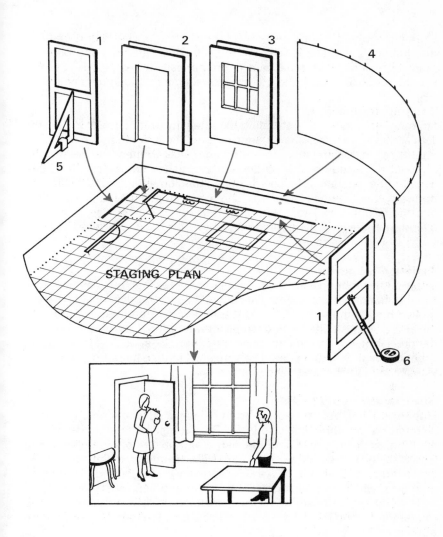

STAGING

Basic staging units

The TV setting is structured from a series of prefabricated units, that can be redecorated and conjoined to build up a wide variety of environments.

   1. Flat.   2. Door flat.   3. Window flat.   4. Cyclorama.   5. Jack.   6. Stage brace.

Aims of Lighting

Lighting is one of those deceptively obvious arts. One might imagine that lighting's first aim is to make the subject visible. And yet there are many occasions when artistically or dramatically this is exactly what we should *not* do, if we want to attract, interest, and intrigue our audience.

Technically speaking
Lighting has always to be of suitable intensity and contrast to suit the TV camera's technical characteristics. One has to arrange the direction, brightness, diffusion (sharpness) and coverage, to meet the artistic and atmospheric needs of the production yet, at the same time, take into account the mechanics involved. The lighting director must consider the nature and directions of cameras' shots, production mechanics, staging, and the facilities available. Although it is possible, of course, to provide overall, generalised illumination by rote, this produces pictures – but with little artistic appeal.

Artistically speaking
Appropriate lighting will model subjects, revealing form, shape, contouring, texture. It can create illusions of space and distance. It can establish environment, building atmospheric effect and mood. Light can develop compositional relationships, creating tonal masses, tonal gradation. Light enables us to draw attention to specific areas, giving prominence or subduing detail selectively. Lighting helps us to maintain visual continuity between shots or scenes.

Basic lighting approaches
Lighting techniques are varied to suit individual situations, but most subjects require three basic sources. The *key-light* is the main luminant, creating modelling, revealing the shape and texture of our subject, and establishing light direction. A *fill light (filler)* is added, a diffused light illuminating the shadows. A *back light,* usually from behind the subject, outlines it with light, helping to create a three-dimensional illusion.

   In addition to these, *set lights* are used selectively to reveal and model the setting (walls, drapes, furniture, etc.) to create an appropriate atmospheric impression.

   The effect of lighting changes with the angles of the illumination, and with the camera's viewpoint. So lighting treatment has to be designed bearing in mind subject movement and direction changes for these alter the appearance of the subject and its surroundings. Consequently, good lighting can only result from imaginative anticipation and systematic planning.

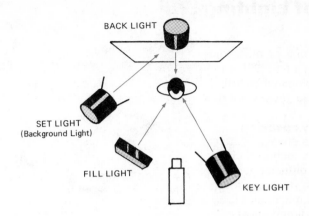

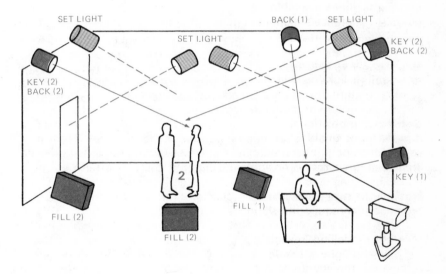

LIGHTING METHODS

Basic lighting treatment
The main *key light*, the diffused *fill light* (that illuminates and softens the shadows), and the *back light*, form the foundation of most lighting treatment.

Complex lighting set-ups
Even a complicated lighting set-up can be analysed into its component parts. Each section 1 and 2, has been lit separately. The key lights, fill lights, back lights and set lights (background lights) are identified here. Sometimes one lamp serves two purposes (eg: 2 key/2 back).

59

Problems of Lighting

Various practical problems can be caused or aggravated by staging and production. These can make lighting arrangements a compromise, or degrade portraiture or picture quality.

Lighting and sound
The presence of the *sound boom* is a major consideration in TV lighting arrangements. The main light *(key light)* is usually located at an angle to the boom arm, to ensure that its shadows are thrown out of shot. But where the mike or boom arm shadows appear in the picture the options are: to move the mike (sound may suffer), to change the lighting (this may affect other shots), to modify the shot (tighten it, or change its angle) or to reposition the performer.

Shadows
Shadows are the essence of dynamic lighting. But when they fall in the wrong place, they become a distraction, or destroy the illusion. Where one performer's shadow falls on another, or on an item he is demonstrating, it is usually easier to reposition people than to re-light. Shadows of a camera may fall onto the subject when shooting from nearby, or high over it, so lighting needs careful angling for such shots.

Subject positions
It is better to avoid locating people close to backgrounds, right in the corner of a room, tucked behind a pillar, or under an overhang (ceiling, arch, beam, or chandelier) for the lighting there is often determined more by the mechanics than by artistic considerations. This is particularly true near pictorial backgrounds (photo blow-ups, rear-projection screens) or perspective structures.

Over-bright surfaces
Excessively bright surfaces *burn out* as blank detailless areas in the picture; whether they are too light in tone, too shiny, or overlit. Sometimes lighting can be adjusted to compensate, but it may be necessary to change the article (white shirts, papers, table coverings), or darken them (spraying or dipping), dulling them (wax spray), or obscuring them.

Precision lighting
The visual effect of any lighting set-up alters with camera viewpoint. Repositioning of subjects or cameras, needs to be taken into account in the lighting treatment. Consequently, if the director makes substantial changes from the originally planned shooting angles, results can be unpredictable, even inferior, unless the lighting happens to be of a very generalised nature. Moreover, any revised lighting treatment may upset earlier parts of the production.

Boom shadows
Boom shadows will usually distract;
particularly if they are moving or
unsteady.

Subject positions
It is well to avoid positioning people
beneath low ceilings.
Placed close to a camera trap, the
camera can see, but lighting is
difficult.
When people sit close to walls, or in
the corners of rooms, close-shooting
cameras may shadow them.
Lighting underneath arches and
overhangs is often poor.

Aims of Make-up

Even in its simplest applications, make-up does untold wonders, both for a performer's visual appeal and for his morale. No experienced director underestimates the value of skilled make-up treatment. He should ensure that the make-up artist has full opportunity to check (preferably on camera) and treat his performers.

Need for make-up
Sometimes a performer's natural complexion, or everyday street make-up, looks fine on the camera, and needs no additional treatment. But most people can benefit from the attentions of a make-up specialist. The work may be minimal – a few touches to neaten the appearance, the wayward hair sticking up at the back, perspiration around temples and brow or the distracting shine on the nose, forehead or a bald head.

There are various blemishes that make a person look a little tired, a little older, perhaps. Make-up can help here, to even out a blotchy complexion, reduce bags under the eyes, improve skin tones or subdue a dark beard line.

Make-up can give vitality and form to a face that the camera shows as rather lacking definition. It can emphasise detail, making eyelashes or the hairline stronger. Subtle shading can enhance the jaw line, chin or nose, to give them clear shape.

Make-up can modify a person's appearance, so that they conform more closely with the current fashion – should that be desirable. But there is always the danger that in so doing, the individual's characteristics may be lost for the sake of a remodelled style. The subtleties of the make-up artist lie in creating effectively naturalistic results. Just as skilled lighting produces realism that is taken for granted, so, after a sensitive 'straight' make-up, the performer looks his best, but still very much himself.

Although it is quite practicable to employ make-up cosmetically (whitening teeth, tautening skin wrinkles, using 'eye conditioner' for a 'clear-eyed' look, and various hair treatments or hair work), this finds less application in everyday television. So too, the most elaborate work of the professional make-up artist (ranging from character creation to monsters) is normally to be found in dramatic roles or special applications, rather than daily programming.

People and make-up
Apart from those few who are, unfortunately, allergic to cosmetics, most performers welcome the personal attention of make-up treatment. Some men may accept it with a certain awareness or embarrassment, but the professional performer is well aware of the importance of effective make-up in the success of his presentation.

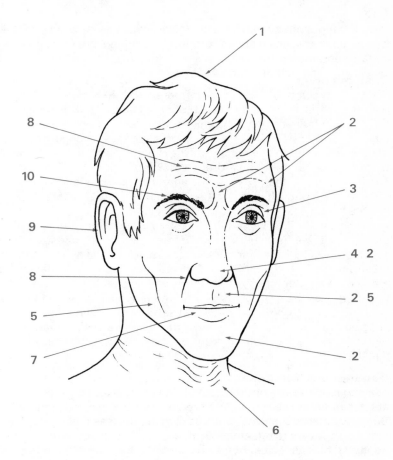

MAKE-UP

Basic make-up improvements

Make-up can help to improve or hide various visual shortcomings:

1. Shiny bald head. Untidy hair. Scalp shows through thin hair. Hair too light, or dark and dense to show well on camera.
2. Perspiration shine.
3. Deep eye sockets. Eyes too prominent. Eyes lack definition.
4. Shiny nose. Nose colouration prominent.
5. Beard-line prominent despite shaving.
6. Neck scrawny.
7. Normal lipstick too light or dark on camera. Lips need definition or shaping.
8. Age-lines, wrinkles, over-prominent.
9. Ears too light; different colour from adjacent skin. Too prominent.
10. Eyebrows untidy; over-prominent; barely discernible.

Wardrobe in TV

The clothing worn by performers in television is, in larger organisations, the general responsibility of a specialist in the costume (wardrobe) department.

Costume origins

For many types of TV show, performers wear their own clothing. They feel at ease in it and they have probably chosen it with thought from their available wardrobe. One needs, therefore, to be sensitive to their feelings and taste, before suggesting that they change any item to make it more suitable on camera. This is particularly true when we want them to wear an item of wardrobe stock (eg: a tinted shirt or a different necktie) because their own is not appropriate. Experienced performers often bring along alternative items of clothing (eg: different coloured sweaters, blouses, ties) for selection on camera.

Some TV stations keep a limited stock of everyday items of clothing that are suitable for general use. Such stock rooms can usually provide satisfactory substitutes for immediate use, as well as augment the basic requirements of more formal or stylised presentations. It may be possible, too, to alter or modify stock items and so enable them to serve multiple purposes. However, it is often more practical for drama (especially period pieces) to hire the necessary attire from costumiers (costume houses), rather than hold stock, or have wardrobe made for the occasion. While a certain amount of workroom creation may be possible, this is not generally an economical solution.

General considerations

Leaving aside aesthetics, and suitability of style for the individual, there are a number of very practical problems in the use of costume on TV. Some are obvious enough, such as clinging dresses that do not permit a girl to sit down elegantly, or at all, in low seats. Others are less apparent, but still quite important. Here are the main considerations:

Avoid tonal extremes in clothing (white shirts or black velvet), for they can appear as unmodelled areas on the screen. Try to have a marked tonal difference between the clothing and background. Remember that what appears as a well-defined contrast in a colour picture may reproduce as areas of similar tonal value in monochrome.

Fine checks, stripes, herringbone and similar patterns in ties, shirts, jackets and dresses are seldom really effective in the TV picture. Detail may be lost, the cloth may appear to vibrate (strobe) against the scanning lines or have colour fringes. Very shiny glossy, sequinned or metallic surfaces can produce startling visual effects that are quite appropriate for 'showbiz' glitter, but not for more everyday applications.

Finally, aim to avoid 'noisy' costume or ornamentations that crackle, rustle, clink or rattle, particularly when personal mikes are being worn.

Background contrast
Aim to have the *tones* of costume
contrast with their background.

Similar patterns
Avoid detailed patterning in both the
foreground and background.

Troublesome close patterns
Close patterns, stripes, checks, will
flicker at certain distances.

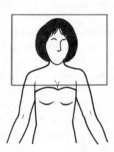

Low neckline problems
Low necklines appear topless in
closer shots.

Need for Production Techniques

In the everyday world, we look around us, watching, interpreting, speculating. So why not let our camera do likewise? In practice, experience shows that *free selection* invariably produces disappointing results, compared with the *guided viewing* that underlies good production techniques.

Why have 'Techniques'?

The size of the TV screen precludes our seeing both detail *and* a broad view simultaneously. A wide lens angle shows more of the scene, but subjects appear smaller. For the audience to look specificially, detail must be sufficiently large and clear, and that inevitably results in a restricted angle of view. Furthermore, if we allow the audience's attention to wander they are less likely to follow coherent, consecutive thought processes. Whether in a drama, newscast, discussion or documentary, we want the viewer to follow the relevant facts closely, if they are to achieve their purpose.

Continuously held shots become boring. To achieve maximum visual interest, and to convey maximum information, we need variation between close shots (of detail), and more distant viewpoints (showing environment, spatial relationships, action, situation, etc.).

Neither a camera nor a mike are replicas of our senses. They modify, interpret, and distort the image they convey of the scene before them (monaural sound, two-dimensional picture, perspective errors, etc.). Because the picture is confined to a flat, rectangular screen, instead of the eye's 'frameless' view of the scene, *apparent* spatial relationships are seen that do not exist. We accept an unreal, flat, black and white TV picture as a reasonable representation of reality, just as we accept considerable colour inaccuracies, and various quite unnatural techniques (dissolves, wipes, inserts, etc.). In other words, the medium is by its very nature *unnatural,* and if used as a semi-static 'observer substitute', soon loses its attraction and appeal for the audience.

Appropriateness of techniques

Creative workers in the film and TV media have developed presentational techniques to both hide and exploit these various limitations. Many are so subtle, or so familiar, that the audience is unaware that techniques or 'manipulations' are actually being used. But these same techniques become intrusions if introduced badly or inappropriately.

'Appropriateness' varies with circumstances and with the individual director's style and subject approach. But many of the fundamental techniques have now become part of the understood grammar of the medium. If these devices are used carelessly, or for their own sake, they destroy the empathy of communication with our audience.

THE SELECTIVE CAMERA

Guided selection

Faced with a crowded, active scene the eye would wander at random if offered
free selection. Guided selection concentrates on local detail or action. In a wide
angle shot, details are so small that they lose individual impact. Spurious factors
distract the attention.

Developing Production Treatment

The successful TV director is, above all, realistic. In deciding on a particular productional approach, he needs to keep in mind a number of factors that may not be immediately obvious.

Established convention
Many kinds of TV production have established formats (eg: quiz games). An audience may welcome a fresh, unconventional presentation, but is equally likely to find it uncomfortably strange and unfamiliar.

Production style
Audience attention soon wanders, especially with a simple and un-dynamic subject that has limited visual appeal. But you must resist the temptation to 'jazz it up' with ingenious shots or visual effects. Clearly, this is a matter of taste. A solitary operatic tenor, pop singer, poet, all provide relatively static subjects requiring different treatment.

Where a show is fast-moving, or has closely reasoned argument or the viewer is required to concentrate on certain points, use closely controlled shots, restricted in coverage and duration.

Talent
The TV experience of performers and contributors to the production must always be considered. Will they have to remember their lines (or points) accurately? Do they need prompters? Or is it a discussion guided by a presenter? Have they precise action or business, moves, timing, that must be repeatable . . . or can we simplify these complications? How experienced and adaptable is the production crew?

Facilities
Always relate the scope and limitations of equipment to the amount and type available. Do not envisage treatment that needs a camera crane, if you have only pedestal mountings! Budget, manpower, time, studio space, regulations (from union rules to fire prevention), and similar hard facts of life must always be considered.

Elaboration of Staging
For many productions, quite simple direct staging is all that is necessary. Fussy, complicated scenic treatment may actually distract attention from the subject. If too basic, though, the effect can look sparse, cheap, amateur and unenterprising – particularly in long shot. But if too elaborately staged, the viewer may take a greater interest in the surroundings than the subject! The setting should give the proper 'weight' to the production, suggesting a sense of occasion, serious or comic.

68

ABOVE THE LINE COSTS
WRITING, PERFORMING, PRODUCTION ELEMENTS

CAST

PERFORMERS

MUSIC • SCRIPT

FLOOR MANAGER

WRITER • SCRIPT EDITOR

CHOREOGRAPHER • MUSICIANS

PRODUCTION PERSONNEL
(PRODUCER DIRECTOR ASSISTANTS)

INSERT MATERIAL (STOCK FILM, ETC.)

OFFICES • REHEARSAL ROOM

ANNOUNCER • OFFICE SERVICES

BELOW THE LINE COSTS
PHYSICAL ELEMENTS INVOLVED IN MOUNTING THE PRODUCTION

MAKE-UP • COSTUMES • GRAPHICS • PROMPTERS

TITLING • TRANSPORTATION • STORAGE • LABOUR

SCENIC DESIGN • SCENERY • CONSTRUCTION • PROPERTIES

STUDIO SERVICING • ENGINEERING PERSONNEL • FILMING

EDITING • VIDEOTAPE RECORDING • REMOTE PICK-UPS (OB's)

SPECIAL EFFECTS • SOUND EFFECTS • STAGE MANAGER

STUDIO FACILITIES AND PERSONNEL (TECHNICAL OPERATIONS CREW
CAMERAS, SOUND, VIDEO, LIGHTING)

ADDITIONAL TECHNICAL FACILITIES ETC. ETC.

PRODUCTION COSTING

The budgeting iceberg
Accurate cost estimation and accounting are essential in television organisation,
despite the great diversity of the various contributions. Budgets are usually
related to the concept of 'above the line', and 'below the line' elements. These
differentiate between the 'writing, performing, and productional elements', and
the various back-up services, and physical elements involved in mounting the
production.

69

Basic Production Methods

Meaningful, persuasive television does not need elaborate methods or facilities. A slow, continuous panning shot over a scene of desolation will convey its extent, and the sheer brooding despair far more significantly than a series of intercut, carefully composed viewpoints.

Formality and informality

Randomly chosen shots have a haphazard influence and lack unity. Purposefully composed shots direct and hold the attention. But meticulously arranged pictures can also appear artificially forced and mannered. They can lack the 'naturalness' of the subjectively used hand-held camera that scrutinises the scene, and zooms in on what interests it. So two philosophies currently run side-by-side in TV production. Where the 'formal method' cuts to an interjecting heckler in a crowd, the 'informal method' may pan around and zoom – even if focus has to be corrected, or the shot wavers. Obviously, the 'informal method' has often stemmed from sheer necessity – if only one camera is present at a real event. But one finds the method introduced in serious drama, too, as the hand-held camera runs, jumps or climbs stairs. Subjectivity encourages audience-involvement – to some degree. It can lead to nausea, too!

Right approach

There is no 'correct' way to present a subject but there are certainly many *wrong* ones! Inappropriate techniques can confuse, mislead, or be ineffectual. Successful methods produce such a smooth continuity of events that the audience becomes oblivious of mechanics. If mechanics intrude, they are being used wrongly – however professionally they have been handled. If the *lay viewer* thinks, 'Boy, what a great zoom!', then he has been affected more by the mechanics than by the programme material. A director can be carried away with his own 'cleverness,' for instance in a sequence of very brief shots cut to the beat of fast music. The result might be fascinating and invigorating – or affectation that does nothing to convey ideas, and merely frustrates the viewer with tantalising glimpses.

Balanced approach

Skilful production involves a blend of *effective audience impact* and selectively organised mechanics. Its pictures and sound guide attention, lay emphasis, influence audience reactions. It is all too easy to become preoccupied with studio mechanics that work – but provide results with a low programmatic value. Conversely, the pictures and sound may be most appropriate – but, due to poor rehearsal, or overambitious aims, the mechanics degenerate, with imprecise switching, camerawork or cueing, and a crudely disrupted presentation results.

Established convention
Would a quiz game look more interesting shot in everyday surroundings?

Instructing talent
Do not preoccupy talent by overloading them with excess instructions.

Know your facilities
Always plan your show with the *available* facilities in mind.

Over-elaborate staging
The setting should be appropriate in content and style to the purpose of the production.

Visual spectacle
Over-ornamentation can pall, and visual novelties need careful handling.

71

Presentational Format

Each *type* of production provides its own particular opportunities and problems. Some shows rest on the performer; elaborate formats would be superficial and intrusive. Others require meticulous planning; each move calculated to interlink with the next. Some involve extremely accurate cueing of inserts. Others challenge one to provide an arresting presentation of what is inherently non-visual subject matter.

Typical formats

Demonstrations are legion, ranging from cookery or auto repairs, to gardening and mountaineering. All concentrate on clarity of detail, show relationships between parts, compare differences in appearance, etc. TV is used as an analytical tool, often freezing or manipulating the speed of action (page 150).

Performance or spectacle involves such diverse subjects as dance, and orchestral concerts. The camera interrelates the broad view, with local shots of detailed action.

Discussion covers all talk-shows (interviews, panels, game shows). The bedrock of live TV, attention divides between speakers and the responses of their companions.

Dramatic presentations, from Shakespeare to soap opera, explore the sophistication of TV grammar – the subtle influences of camerawork, editing, sound, lighting, etc.

Composite presentations such as current affairs or documentary programmes, intersperse studio material (commentator, experts, graphics) with inserted film, videotape or slides. Precise cueing and timing are essential.

Compilation programmes blend together excerpts from a series of other shows, or from library (stock) material and are usually designed to survey, summarise, or recapitulate subjects.

Remotes (Outside broadcasts, OBs) televised from a point outside the studio centre, are usually very limited in the variety of treatment they can provide. Facilities are fewer than in the studio, and there is less opportunity for complex camera operations. Large areas and distances often have to be covered, despite restricted viewpoints, terrain and weather problems, etc.

Live versus recorded presentation

Most TV shows today are video-recorded, rather than transmitted as they happen *(live)*. Fault-free continuous transmission of anything more than the simplest production requires careful organisation, close teamwork, and 'first-time' reliability. Recording, on the other hand, permits retakes and rearrangements, and post-production decisions, so that precision results can often be achieved from shows originally containing errors and misjudgements.

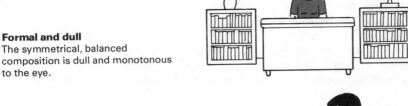

Formal and dull
The symmetrical, balanced composition is dull and monotonous to the eye.

Posed shots
Composition has been carefully arranged here for dramatic effect. It could be mannered and too obviously arranged, or a powerful, naturally-evolved composition for the subject in hand.

Arranged display
The pattern the dancers make adds to the visual appeal of the presentation.

Contrived pattern
The seated speakers, sitting in an identical pattern, look inappropriately arranged. The effect is awkward and strange.

Do not underestimate single-camera opportunities.

Using Only One Camera

Although one tends to think of continuous TV production as essentially a multi-camera process, single-camera treatment is sometimes unavoidable. A director may be on location with a single-camera unit (video or film), or must shoot studio action with a single mounting, others being dispersed or isolated.

At first sight, it might be assumed that a single TV camera can only provide very restricted productional opportunities. In reality, with careful planning and a little ingenuity, very effective presentations can be devised, especially for localised or single-subject situations.

Subject movement
Even where the camera does not move at all, the presentation need not be unduly static. Movement can be introduced by having the performer change his position, walking around within the scene, transferring interest from one area to the next. If the centres of attention are arranged at different distances from the camera, variations in shot size are achieved without altering the lens angle or camera position. In a display situation, larger subjects can be placed further from the camera position, and small subjects for close-up shots, on a foreground table. A small turntable could be used to rotate an item and show its various aspects. Occasionally, you might *pull focus* between subjects to transfer audience attention.

Camera movement
If the camera position may be changed, and the lens judiciously zoomed a single camera seems far less restrictive. Shot-size, and viewpoint can be readily adjusted. The performer can move, and the camera follow. He looks down to pick up an item, and the camera tilts and zooms with his hand to a close shot, as he reaches out to take hold of it.

Using inserts
Where only one camera is available, therefore (even if it is static), fluid production techniques are still possible. Treatment does not have to degenerate into simply zooming and panning around. By cutting away to inserts (graphics, film or VT inserts), flexibility can be further extended by giving time for camera repositioning, shot changes, etc.

Editing
When videotaping a production, editing can simulate the flexibility of a multi-camera production – intercutting repeat takes with different sized shots taken from varying viewpoints. That is, after all, precisely how many motion pictures are shot – using a single film camera. Tape editing is, however, relatively more laborious, and inter-camera switching produces an end product more rapidly.

74

SUBJECT MOVEMENT

Equidistant positions
Items here are arranged equidistant from the camera, to provide a succession of similar shots as the talent moves across the scene. This treatment is useful when dealing with a number of objects of comparable size.

Movement in depth
Here the items are arranged in depth relative to the oblique camera viewpoint. The talent moves towards the camera, and the size of shot changes. This treatment is particularly useful when objects of various sizes are being shown.

Multi-camera Production

A single camera obliges us to organise our treatment carefully, to make the most of limited facilities.

Benefits of the second camera
A second camera provides us with an opportunity for immediate visual change. In an instant, we can alter shot size or switch to a new viewpoint. We do this to provide fresh information, to alter emphasis, to point new detail, to compare relationships, or to provide visual variety.

During a single-camera show, we may find ourselves having to change shot for mechanical reasons (eg: a dolly or zoom back to enable the frame to accommodate another person). Where we have a second camera, we do not have to introduce these superfluous mechanics. However, there are potential pitfalls too! If we have more than one camera, there are more preview pictures to keep an eye on, more people to instruct, a greater chance of getting another camera in shot, or of cutting to the wrong source!

Elaboration becomes possible
With a second camera available, the director can take *reaction shots* and *cutaway shots* during the action (instead of taking material for cut-ins afterwards). In a two-camera set-up, one can take wider overall shots, while the other concentrates on close-ups.

When appropriate, we may even show both the shots (or parts of them) from both cameras simultaneously, using superimposition, split-screen, insets or vignettes.

Where visual effects are involved (a diffused image, or multi-image lens, perhaps), these can be fitted to one camera, while the other provides normal pictures.

Multi-camera shooting
Multi-camera shooting provides not simply a method for creating pictorial variety, but a means of shifting audience attention rapidly, or making immediate comparisons. Multi-camera work simplifies the mechanics of continuous production. In a *single camera* production, the action must generally be confined to one contiguous area. Using a *second camera,* action can be separated, and near the end of a two-camera scene, one can be released to move in readiness to the next action area. Using a *third camera,* shot availability is extended. We can, for example, cover the main set with Cam. 1, supported by Cam. 2, while Cam. 3 shoots graphics or floor captions and titles and provides opening shots in new action areas. Where scenes are short, as in 'one-liner' comic sketches, cameras may have to move and interchange between areas very rapidly. Likewise in fast or widespread action, one soon uses all available cameras, in providing sufficient coverage.

76

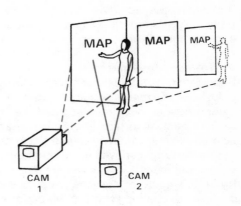

Two-camera treatment
Shots are divided between the two cameras. Cam. 1 concentrates on wider-angle shots. Cam. 2 takes close-ups of maps and speaker.

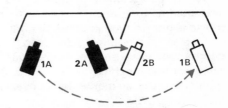

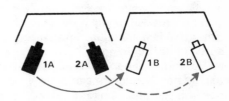

Maximum use of cameras
One camera to each set is unnecessarily restrictive.
Near the end of a two-camera scene, Cam. 2 pans to the next area. Cameras can move away successively. Cam. 2 moves first (A – B); Cam. 1 joins it.

Avoid static set-ups.

Changing Shot – Moving Performer

It is all too easy to devise presentations that consist of little more than intercut 'pot-shots' from static viewpoints. But for interest and visual appeal, movement and change are essential.

Performer movement

Suppose someone just stands at a table, pointing out details in a series of articles. Movement is slight, but even this is preferable to absolutely static shots, as with intercut slides. He moves across the scene and the camera pans with him (preferably in a mid or long shot). The viewer now has a sense of environment (location, scale, mood).

The performer moves up to the camera, and two things happen. The viewer becomes more aware of scenic depth on a movement to (or from) the camera, and the emphasis changes from the dominating environment (in long shot) to the performer himself (in the close shot).

There are several ways in which a person can be arranged to give a natural, visually motivated opportunity to change a shot. He can, of course, *walk* from one item to another, and this shifts attention from one action area to the next. He can make a *gesture* – eg: pointing over to a feature that the camera pans to see. Or, as he turns in a close-up, the camera can use the *body turn* to pan or zoom towards the new subject (page 74). A *verbal reference* ('Over there we have . . .') is an open invitation for the shot to change.

Group shots

Fundamentally, we can create shot variations in two ways.

When using *isolating shots,* the lens angle of each camera is restricted so that it selects one or two people, and excludes the others. These shots are then intercut, to obtain variation.

Instead of maintaining the main group, and seeking shots within it, it can be broken up selectively, *regrouping* people into two-shots etc . . . This is done by introducing 'natural' moves, business, and visually motivated cuts, as mentioned above. Here is an example:

> Within a group shot, a person turns away in annoyance during an argument (illustration opposite) and becomes a single shot; meanwhile, his puzzled companion looks towards a third person, and forms a two-shot.

Such repositioning now provides an entirely fresh series of shot opportunities, that just intercutting between isolating shots within a static group could not.

By moving people around *within the frame,* the compositional balance of the picture can be altered, and so shift the emphasis as they rise, sit or alter posture. Because movement attracts attention, it 'covers' the shift of interest.

78

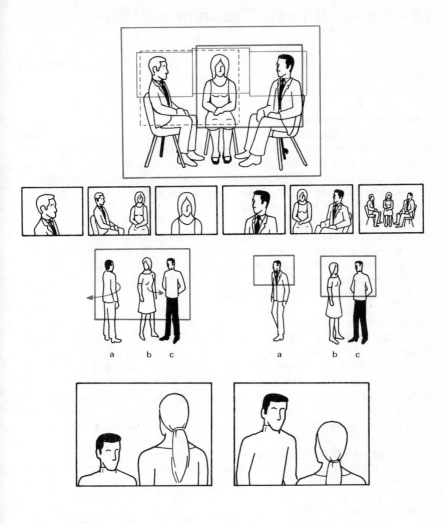

MOVING PERFORMERS

Forming shots by isolation
Where people are grouped, and cameras segment the scene into single shots, two-shots, etc., the result is a rather static presentation.

Forming shots by subject movement
People can move 'naturally' to form new groupings. Here, in a three-shot, Person a. turns away; we cut to CU of him. Person b. looks towards c., to motivate a two-shot.

Recomposition by subject movement
The girl confronts her father (her frame position is stronger than his). He rises; the strength of his upward move and new position now make him dominant.

Changing Shot – Camera and Switching

Some situations are necessarily immobile, and variety has to come from camera movement and switching.

Changes by camerawork
The simplest visual change that can be made in a static situation, is to *tighten or loosen the shot* – by zooming or dollying (tracking) the camera. This may be done to reframe the picture and permit or exclude action, such as arm movements. Or if someone exits, or joins the shot it may deliberately change emphasis. Again, we may want to go in to see detail, or pull out to reveal more of the scene.

Instead of changing the picture by altering shot size, it can sometimes be done by adjusting *camera height.* However, this must usually be during movement (as a person sits or rises) otherwise the change can be intrusive. So, too, the camera can *arc round* a subject to gain a new viewpoint. But unless there is clear motivation, the effect can appear cumbersome on a stationary subject.

Changes by switching
Switching to another camera, immediately alters the shot size *(length of shot),* or relocates the audience's viewpoint. Whenever these are done simultaneously, there is a risk of disorientation, for a moment at least, especially if the changes are extreme. Where the dialogue or story line prepares the viewer for change, though, even extreme switches can be quite acceptable (eg: to an overhead shot, or an entirely new location). But, unprepared, an audience may be confused, especially if a different speaker is involved in the new shot.

Two very practical hazards encountered in switching are *reverse cuts* (page 81) and *re-discoveries.* Keep an eagle eye for these when arranging shots as they are disturbing to watch.

Static subjects
Where the subject is completely inanimate (eg: a vase, statue), there are several techniques for increasing its visual appeal. A hand can come into shot to handle the object (so revealing scale). A rotating turntable can present its various facets. Appearance can be altered considerably with lighting variations – ranging from silhouette to texture-revealing side-lighting. We can light localised areas, gradually showing more until it becomes fully illuminated – As intractable a subject as a painting can be treated in this way. One can even create pseudo-animation by camera movement on a static illustration.

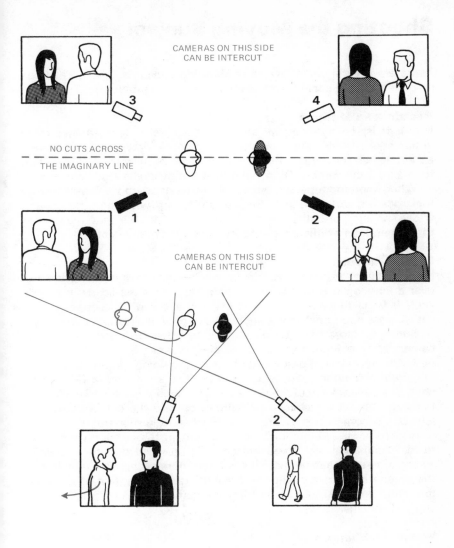

CAMERAS ON THIS SIDE
CAN BE INTERCUT

NO CUTS ACROSS
THE IMAGINARY LINE

CAMERAS ON THIS SIDE
CAN BE INTERCUT

EFFECTS ON SWITCHING

Reverse cuts

Shots can be intercut between cameras located on the same side of an *imaginary line* joining the subjects (1 and 2. 3 and 4.). Inter-switching between cameras on *opposite* sides of this line, causes the positions of subjects to jump (1 and 3. 1 and 4. 2 and 3. 2 and 4.).

Rediscoveries

If a person exits the frame, it is disconcerting to switch and rediscover them in the next shot. Leave Cam. 1 shot, he reappears on Cam. 2.

Not as obvious as it looks.

Shooting the Moving Subject

There are several distinct ways of shooting moving subjects. Each has its own audience impact, and its own operational problems.

Restrictions of frame
If a shot is too *tight* for the amount of subject movement, we must either take a wider shot, or alter the camera viewpoint. Remember, action across the screen moves out of frame more quickly than action to and from the camera. Diagonal moves are generally more interesting.

When shooting a person who is about to stand up we have to avoid their passing out of frame. So we can tilt up with their movement, widen the shot, or cut to a wider view. The tighter the shot, the greater the cameraman's difficulties in following erratic movement.

Camera moves
It can be easier to pan with a moving person than to dolly alongside him over a long walk. However, when panning across-the-scene in a wide shot, it is all too easy to 'over-pan', and shoot off the edges of the set – unless appropriate masking has been provided near its edges.

Some directors have coped with 'long walks' by cutting to a new camera at an oblique angle as the subject moves off. The action moves up to the new viewpoint instead of across the scene. Unfortunately, this ploy can look rather odd, when the result is a cut from a fairly close shot, to a distant view of the same person – who proceeds to walk up to the new camera to achieve a picture rather like the one we have just left! One becomes over-aware of the mechanics in such treatment.

Instead of following somebody's movement throughout, we can cut to his destination and await his coming, provided that the viewer is aware of what is happening. This is often more acceptable than letting the person move out of shot before cutting. The *direction* of the walk, too, can matter. A walk away from the camera, for instance, tends to suggest conclusion of action.

Viewpoint changes
When organising his camera treatment, a director must always take into account how smoothly and reliably these moves can be carried out. A camera can *creep* imperceptibly closer to a subject while holding a shot. A slow zoom is easier than a *dolly (tracking)* shot, and may suffice instead. *Pulling-out* requires rather more skill, and care must be taken not to include spurious objects nearby as the shot widens. *Arcing* round a subject demands practised camerawork, particularly if the subject itself is not stationary.

Remember that where a person and a camera are both moving, close coordination is essential, so that the speed of a walk. for example, should be comparable during rehearsals and recording.

82

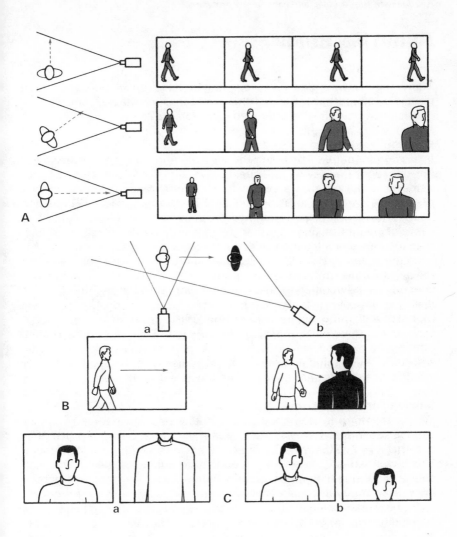

THE MOVING SUBJECT

A. Movement direction
Movements across the screen (a) quickly pass out of shot. Diagonal moves (b), or moves towards the camera (c) can be sustained longer.

B. Oblique angles
Movement between widely-spaced subjects can only be accommodated on an oblique camera (b).

C. Avoid decapitation
Warn the cameraman of a 'rise' or a 'sit', and avoid bizarre effects.

Avoid Routines

Many regular forms of TV presentation have developed their own particular stereotypes. But are these methods inevitable? Are they inherent? How can they be improved – or replaced?

Routine treatments

Interviews (page 158) in the form; mid-shot of interviewer (introduction), mid-shot of guest, two-shot, intercut close-ups of whoever is talking, plus a switch to occasional reaction shots follow a predictable pattern. Can it be avoided? *TV Drama* (page 172) has had its routines, too: an overall *establishing shot* (to show the locale); group shots of people talking together (to reveal or establish relationships); cuts to close shots when individuals speak, allowing sufficient room for movement and gestures, with reaction shots added for good measure; moving to wider shots to see the entrance of a newcomer, and a close-shot of the newcomer to assist identification and recognition. If the dialogue is overlong, *business* is introduced to break up visual monotony (lighting cigarettes, getting drinks from table downstage, leaning on mantlepiece, sitting down, etc.). This is routine drama, offering mechanical solutions to artistic problems. Watch a TV serial with this idea in mind and see if you recognise its basic application – or whether the director has used his cameras creatively.

Non-routine treatments

Where the format of a show has virtually become decreed by convention (as in quiz game layouts) treatment variations can prove difficult (pages 71, 90, 171). TV directors have striven hard to find them. The 'walk-about' interview, conducted while strolling through countryside, down a street, or in a factory, was a method of getting away from the ever-familiar studio set-up. It was an innovation – once.

So how does one get away from routine presentation? Opinions vary. Many directors do so by introducing variety. They vary camera heights and viewpoints. They use developing shots rather than static 'pot-shots'. Any *business* appears to be in character, and naturally activated – eg: a gardener cleaning tools as he talks. The shots chosen are particularly purposeful and appropriate to the situation or mood – for example for quicker intercutting during tense moments.

In using more imaginative treatment, however, avoid introducing shots that are merely eccentric, mannered or bizarre. The list of these grows daily: reflections (shots taken via a reflective surface), shots into the sun (with or without star filters), 'fidget shots' of fingers intertwining, straightening ties, drumming fingers, tapping feet, etc., over-use of big close-ups of guests under questioning, too many over-shoulder shots, shots peering through foreground foliage and so on. Fashions come and go, as in all things!

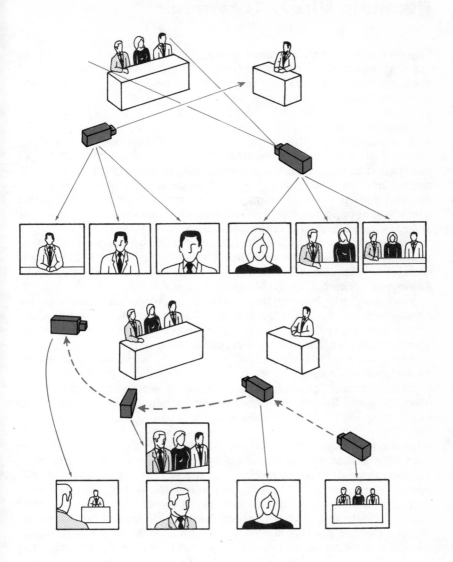

SHOOTING METHODS

Static shooting
Where cameras are located at *fixed* vantage points and achieve shot variations only by changing lens-angles, regular routine treatments often develop.

Dynamic shooting
Where camera positions are *varied* to provide viewpoint changes, repetitive shots are readily avoided.

Do not wait to work it all out on the day!

Planning Visual Treatment

There tend to be two fundamental approaches to visual treatment. In the first, the director begins with the mechanics of the situation, and derives effective shots. In the second, he conceives effective shots, and arranges the mechanics to provide them.

Planned viewpoints
This is undoubtedly the commonest approach for many types of TV show. The cameras are located strategically near the action, in positions that experience has shown to offer optimum shot variations. A pattern of front-central and cross-cutting cameras is typical. Shots are devised from these viewpoints. At its best, this arrangement provides useful visual opportunities, and ensures operational continuity (there is always a camera ready for the next shot).

Frequently, the strategy is for each camera to be allocated particular types of shots. For instance, Cam. 1 takes cover shots of a group of dancers, while Cam. 2 and Cam. 3 take close-ups of individuals. Cameras are intercut, using this shooting pattern.

Well handled, this method of visual treatment can provide very satisfactory, workmanlike results. It takes minimum rehearsal effort, and is readily coordinated, for the crew members recognise their roles, and concentrate on achieving clear, uncluttered shots.

At its simplest, this approach can lead to a procedure in which cameramen offer up 'good shots' and the switcher cuts to the best or most appropriate. Cutting is more a way of transferring attention, than a dramatic tool. The results may be quite adequate. But pictures can easily prove unrelated and haphazard.

Storyboard approach
Less widely used, the *storyboard approach* requires careful systematic forethought and coordinated planning. It is concerned with *shot significance.* The director considers the points he wants to make in a particular shot, arranges the picture (in his mind, or in rough sketches) to encapsulate this idea, then works out the mechanics he requires to achieve this composition and overall effect. Then he must consider how he will in practical terms, get from one shot to the next (eg: moving the camera, subject, adding business, cutting to a new viewpoint, etc.). Working progressively through the show, breaking it down into its component parts, the shots become scenes or sequences expressing particular dramatic ideas, attracting the audience to specific aspects of the subject and the scene. Emphasis is controlled, mood is engendered. Editing contributes to the impact of the presentation.

But such an approach takes time, patience and empathy. Instead, directors often have to use a series of storyboard *key shots,* and develop intermediary shots as planned viewpoints.

86

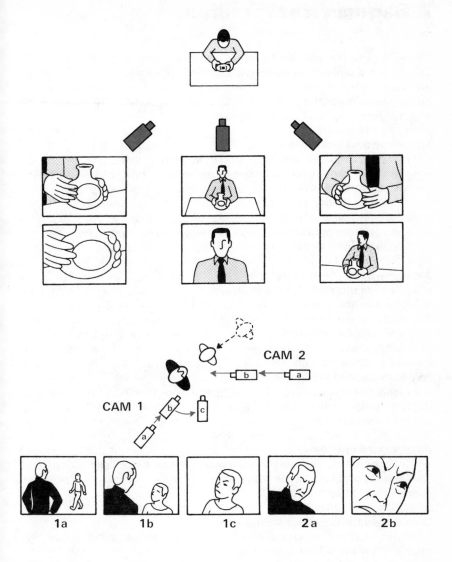

VISUAL TREATMENT

Planned viewpoints
Cameras are placed in positions from which they can get clear shots of the
action. Their pictures are intercut as required.

Storyboard approach
A dramatic action sequence is conceived as a series of sketched frames. The
camera treatment is then devised to provide these pictures.

A Sequence of Pictures

When we conjoin a series of shots, we interrelate them, building up a group significance, suggesting a space/time relationship, even when none exists. (Eg: CU of scared man, cut to snarling lion. We assume that he is reacting to the animal.) This effect is particularly pronounced when intercutting brief duration shots.

Rapid cutting
However, any director in the TV studio who seeks to use this effect, encounters problems. Film can conjoin an endless variety of shots at any working rate. But when rapidly interswitching TV cameras, the cutting rate can outrun the cameraman's ability to set up new shots. Rather than rapid cutting, therefore, the TV director more usually relies on subject and camera movement to alter shots, and give pictorial variations. Using TV cameras, shots tend to be held longer.

Extending shot flexibility
Using videotape editing, or film inserts, there are virtually no immediate limits to the shot variations available to us. But working in real time in the studio, the director may feel that his shot flexibility is limited. There is insufficient time to move a camera, or no floor-space to shoot an item properly, or a particular camera move is not likely to be smooth. Here foresight and a certain amount of ingenuity can help. Some typical solutions are shown opposite. If you have a succession of brief shots of a series of articles, why not place them equidistant from a couple of cameras, intercutting as each pans rapidly on to the next? Or you could intercut a series of pull-out photographs. If space causes a camera to be too close to its subject, it could gain distance by shooting via a mirror. If a camera has no room to arc round an object, why not put that object on a turntable, and rotate it instead? Frustrations can become a challenge! Cameras may achieve shot flexibility by exploring projected slides.

Subject and objective treatments
When the camera moves around, the impact tends to be *subjective,* representing the viewer's relationship to the scene. The camera moves in to peer at detail. The performer addresses his audience directly, perhaps bringing objects up to the camera so that we can see them more clearly. In general, we can say that subjective techniques involve the audience more completely than objective ones, but demand more controlled camera operation.

Used *objectively,* the camera becomes a more detached onlooker, like, an observer watching the action from a good vantage point. Here, intercut viewpoints would normally be used instead of camera movement.

METHODS OF RAPID SHOT CHANGE

Quick pans
Rapid intercutting is possible, if cameras pan quickly between equidistant items.

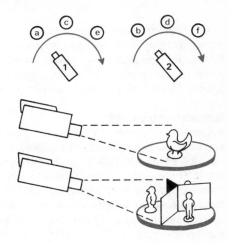

Turntables
Turntables enable various aspects to be seen easily, or to provide rapidly changed displays.

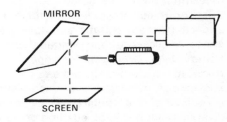

Front projected slides
A compact device for projecting and shooting slides uses a 45° mirror.

MIRROR

SCREEN

Instant repositioning
With a quick pan to a mirror, the camera is virtually repositioned to a new viewpoint.

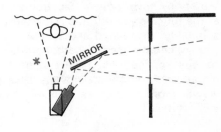

MIRROR

Pull-out graphics
Using a series of pull-out graphics in a grooved box, rapid changes are possible.

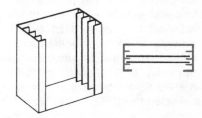

'Variety' is not welcome for its own sake.

Visual Variety

The director aims to attract and maintain audience interest, concentrating and relaxing attention as the production material requires. By doing this, he avoids sameness, repetition, or a recognisable pattern pervading the show. Instead of a predictable routine, his production develops individual character and appeal.

Introducing variety

Variety by decor: Where a production involves an inherently stereotyped presentation (page 84), variety must be introduced through novelty of decor, rather than through imaginative production techniques. The setting looks different, but the shots conform to the format that experience has found to be optimum for effective presentation. Productions for which this applies include newscasts, orchestral concerts, open-stage song and dance, talks and interviews.

Variety by movement: Whether moving the subject or the camera, this movement should be purposeful, clearly motivated, and relevant (page 38). Too much movement, or fidgety, contrived action (to get variety into an inherently static situation, pages 78, 157), is more likely to annoy an audience than intrigue them.

Variety by changes in viewpoint and shot sizes: Appropriately introduced, such changes create a sense of visual freedom for our audience. A restricted, over-used viewpoint, can make them extremely conscious of the confines of the small screen. Changes that are too diverse, though, can be puzzling or distracting (page 80).

Variety by novel effects: Electronic wizardry provides endless gimmicks at the touch of a button, but the temptation is to use them regardless of suitability. Combined shots, multi-images, superimpositions and split screen, can be used to demonstrate scale, spatial relationships, etc., in serious applications. They can be used to show someone singing to himself in a show-biz novelty presentation. Novelties can make the viewer more curious as to how it was done than concerned with the subject itself!

Unconventional approach

Unusual presentation for its own sake, however intriguing, may look mannered. A current routine is to take a close shot of foreground flowers (with no significance), and then pull focus to see the real subject (eg: hero's escaping car) in the distance. This is simply an obtrusive trick, conveying nothing. But to pull focus from foreground barbed wire, to prisoners beyond, could establish a powerful symbolic association. It is a matter of appropriateness. Foreground borders similarly can add depth and set location, or appear posed and prearranged.

Pictorial variety
By the ways in which we arrange people in a shot, we can create visual variety, concentrate attention, and suggest prevailing mood.

Shot Development

One of the problems encountered by an inexperienced director, is that he arranges a good shot but then, on cutting to another viewpoint, finds that his new shot is unacceptable. An adjustment in the new shot may spoil composition in the first. Clearly, in continuous production the interplay of viewpoints cannot be taken for granted.

Viewpoint changes

When we *move* a camera from one viewpoint to another, visual continuity is ensured. When we *switch* to another viewpoint, there is always the possibility of disturbing compositional changes (page 49). There are two ways of achieving good composition in consecutive shots. Firstly, we can use *equalised viewpoints;* positioning subjects so that they look right from both directions. This requires anticipatory planning (pages 159, 161), or experiment during rehearsals.

Secondly, we can *readjust people's positions* as the shot changes – rather as we did to separate people from a group on page 78. Here we move them to change the composition. We do this by setting up the first shot, then readjusting it to suit the second viewpoint. The dialogue at the transition point serves as a *word cue* (page 120) for an actor to move from the first position to the second. In practice, one 'motivates' the move. A person sits, or has some rational 'business' (eg: puts down a glass). The change may be implied in the dialogue 'Come in'. . . he turns towards door.

So strong is the sense of continuity when change is motivated in these ways, that we can conjoin action that is in different places, or is not concurrent for example, a character looks out of a window and says, 'There he goes' . . . cut to a film shot of person walking down a street. A relationship has been created that does not really exist!

Continuous development

Developing shots (development shots) explore the scene. The camera moves within it, helping the audience to build up an impression of space, distance or layout. It creates a subjective impression of involvement, rather than surveying the scene from the sidelines (page 88).

Developing shots require skilled, carefully controlled camerawork, for they entail continuous adjustment of framing and focus, with accurate dolly movement (while avoiding obstacles).

The amount and extent of movement must, of course, be consistent with the *pace (tempo)* and mood of the occasion. It is usually slow, for developing shots are mostly used in scenes where tension or expectancy is high, or on solemn occasions, or during romantic episodes.

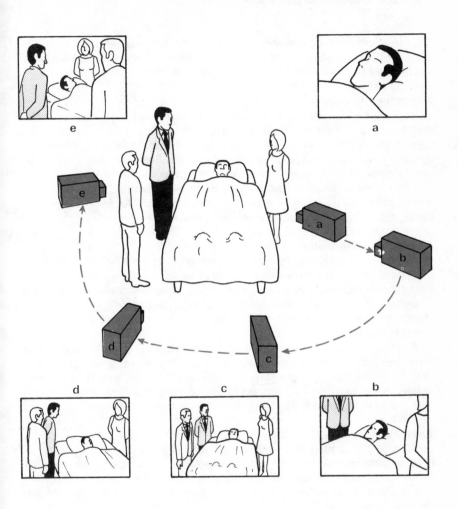

DEVLEOPING SHOT

Developing shot
In this bedside scene, intercutting would have disrupted the solemn mood. And yet one wants to show various reactions, and create continuous visual interest. This slow developing shot provides movement, unobtrusive, yet contrasting with the stillness of the scene.

What Facilities Are Needed?

The wise director conceives his show with the available facilities in mind. For it is far better to start from basic needs, and build up ideas as elaboration becomes necessary, or lends point to the show.

A matter of degree
Most subjects can be presented in a variety of ways. Some approaches may be more attractive, or more effective than others. Their appeal may vary, but so will their budget needs. For example, a programme on warfare could be handled simply as a narration. But we could add library stills and film clips, devise special graphics, make studio miniatures to show the battle layout, have specially animated film, introduce studio drama or even reconstruct events with actual location mammoth battle scenes! Budgets usually temper ambitions!

Alternative methods
A particular visual effect can then be achieved by several quite different methods. Some are easier or more flexible to use than others. A high shot that would really need a camera crane, may be obtained by putting a camera on an elevated area (parallels, rostra, frame tower), by shooting into a suspended mirror, or even by cutting to a photo-still taken earlier.

A special facility used for one brief shot alone is usually wasteful of time and effort. But a whole scene might require special treatment, such as shots from ground level throughout. If so, are special low-level dollies necessary, or can the problem be overcome by arranging the action on an elevated area, and using normal floor pedestals?

Tempting facilities
Various facilities have become widely available, so that the temptation is to use them — because they are there. Resist the temptation! Think twice before using a *wipe, whip-pan, zoom, star filters, superimposition, synthesised colour.* They may all be there at the touch of a switch, but are they *appropriate*?

What does the viewer see?
The audience cares little about how difficult or costly it is to achieve a given shot. They are only concerned with the *effect*. If the camera looks through a doorway and apparently sees a room interior, it is not important that this 'room' is really only made from a couple of scenic flats. Carefully chosen camera viewpoints can prove economical in staging and facilities. Judiciously used chroma-key (CSO page 152) too, can provide elaborate effects with minimum staging. Although such approaches may preclude interesting developing shots, they can provide considerable visual variety.

94

Coping Without Facilities

Too few Cameras: Restrict action areas. End scene on one camera, releasing others to next area (page 77). Videotape each section/scene separately, using available cameras. Introduce cutaway shots to slides or graphics, film, or videotape, while changing camera positions. See pages 74, 76.

Cameras Immobile: Intercut between static camera (page 74). Rely on subject movement to vary shots. Have performers work to cameras. Cut to photographs/slides of detail. Use videotape/film inserts. Arrange series of action areas equidistant from camera (page 89). Pan to shoot via a mirror.

Lens Angle Fixed: Vary distance of action from camera (page 74). Move camera relative to action. Fit supplementary lens.

Insufficient Time to Move a Camera: Add extra action/-business/dialogue, to extend scene while camera moves. Insert cutaway shot to relevant graphics slides, etc.

Limited Space: Use partial settings (only localised area built, to suggest an extensive scene). Use wide-angle lenses to exaggerate space. Re-vamp sets (change appearance) while off camera. Use chroma-key, or front projection, or realistic backdrops (backings). Cover windows with nets or blinds, and avoid using room doors (no backings then needed). Shoot via a mirror. Introduce false perspective. Intercut between separate areas of similar decor (so suggesting scenic continuity).

Limited Staging Resources: Re-vamp settings. Use adaptable/reversible scenery. Use chroma-key. Use a cyclorama as background (light patterns, tonal changes, etc.). Use drapes.

Limited Lighting Facilities: Confine staging areas. Record scene-by-scene. Use chroma-key or front projection. Simulate scenic lighting (shade the wall tones). Paint 'window shadows'.

No Slide (Film) Scanner: Use studio TV camera to shoot the image projected onto a shielded screen.

Is Planning Really Necessary?

A TV show *can* be directed 'off-the-cuff' devising the shots spontaneously without detailed planning. In a recurrent daily talks show, for example, the treatment may be mostly repetitious, and the crew very familiar with the formula. But any 'one-off' production needs planning, unless its format fits an elementary pattern. Unpredictability is not adventurous. It can degenerate into a worrying muddle.

Teamwork
We are presenting the audience with audio-visual stimuli. If our show has rational development, and is coherent they react to these along reasonably predictable lines. Random, or ill-chosen stimuli produce haphazard, ambiguous, puzzling results. Furthermore, because TV is the work of a group of separate contributors, we have to ensure that their individual efforts are coordinated. (It is all too easy to have a guest in a discussion speak – when all the cameras have shots elsewhere.) Without coordination, operational faults arise, shots go astray, sound and pictures are distractingly bad, items fail to arrive or don't work. Organise your presentation so that everyone knows what is expected of them, and when. Overplanning can provide a precise, soulless product. But few shows are overplanned!

When forward planning is impractical
Planning is not only a practical necessity, but it disciplines the director to think out exactly how he is going to present his subject. At the least, he must arrange an outline, showing the sets, action areas, principal positions of cameras and sound booms, floor graphics, and list associated contributory facilities (slides, film, VTR inserts).

Even in an unavoidably impromptu show, there should be a general idea of its nature and flow pattern, and a basic treatment (page 160). The format should be explained to the crew. This procedure can be rehearsed on camera using stand-ins, if possible, with the crew noting the rehearsed version on 'blank scripts'. Even this tentative approach is preferable to any attempt to 'make it up on the day'.

Planning meetings
For productions of any complexity, a technical planning meeting well in advance of the studio date is essential. At this meeting, the specialists responsible for the various visual and audio aspects of the show listen to the director giving details of his presentation ideas. They in turn offer their individual expertise, evaluate and extend his ideas, anticipate problems, etc., and subsequently organise their own contributions to his treatment (pages 98, 99).

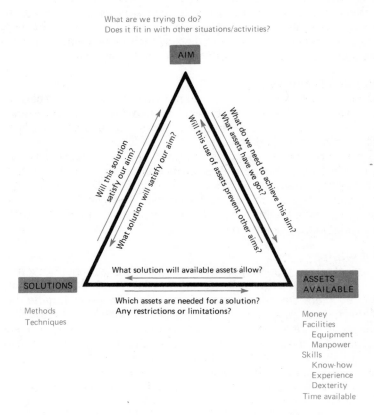

What are we trying to do?
Does it fit in with other situations/activities?

AIM

Will this solution satisfy our aim?

What solution will satisfy our aim?

What do we need to achieve this aim?
What assets have we got?

Will this use of assets prevent other aims?

What solution will available assets allow?

SOLUTIONS

ASSETS AVAILABLE

Which assets are needed for a solution?
Any restrictions or limitations?

Methods
Techniques

Money
Facilities
 Equipment
 Manpower
Skills
 Know-how
 Experience
 Dexterity
Time available

HOW TO PLAN

The planning process
The problem is *where to begin!* This 'universal problem-solving circuit' helps us to think coherently about planning procedures. Whenever we have a problem, we must relate any potential solution to our assets, or the result will be unsuccessful. Note how the circuit works clockwise and anti-clockwise. There is often no *correct* solution, only an optimum for our needs.

Organising Production Mechanics

Planning and organising processes vary from one establishment to the next. In a small studio, everyone combines forces to build the show, and job demarcations are slight. At a larger studio centre, inter-departmental and union relationships are usually clear-cut, and a con-siderable amount of documentation is necessary for the wheels to turn. Whatever the system, the people who are going to provide the various facilities and services still have to discuss their respective ideas. The list on the facing page is a reminder of the scope for discussion.

Production resources

However experienced, a director cannot hope to know the answers to the thousand and one aspects that arise when devising a TV show. That is why he has expert advice from specialists. Some apparently difficult requirements are remarkably easy to meet (such as a shot of a man suddenly shrinking to become minute), while paradoxically, some 'simple' situations can pose real problems as for example obtaining convincing open-air acoustics in large-area studio scenes. So the director consults his aides on how to obtain a convincing illusion, how to save money and time, how a setting can be modified to offer a better variety of shots and so on.

Will it work?

In practical terms, planning usually prompts the questions: What are we trying to achieve? How can we accomplish this? Will that method work? Are there any potential problems? How do we overcome these? Was the idea a good one in the first place? Many a 'great idea' has proved to be a confounded nuisance to other contributing specialists, or an unworkable fiasco on the studio floor. The more we can anticipate and rationalise at the planning stage, the better.

Take a simple example of aspects discussed for a scene:

> *A girl walks upstairs, speaking throughout the walk.* How is the camera shooting the walk? It is tilting up from a position at the foot of the stairs. Will the camera shoot off the top of the set? No, there is a ceiling. Will this ceiling preclude appropriate lighting? No, it can be effectively lit from these other directions. If a sound boom is to follow the walk, the boom operator will not be able to see from the suggested position. Then a flat must be moved to give him a clear view. The mike might be seen in the long shot. Can't the mike work further away for that shot? The sound quality (acoustics) will change, particular-ly due to the low ceiling. Let's see if it is too bad, or if we have to use other sound pick-up methods. Will the footsteps on the stairs sound authentic? They are thickly carpeted, so that should be all right.

Camera-cable routing, too, is a potential hazard. Cables can get snarled up, or block other cameras' moves, or drag around making noises. Many directors therefore move scale cut-outs on cords around their *staging plan,* to ascertain problems, before allocating camera positions for their *camera plan.*

Typical Considerations in Technical Planning

Talent: Cast discussed, re costume and make-up requirements (styles, fitting arrangements, etc.).

Staging: Designer outlines proposed style, treatment of settings. Staging plan, details of set structures, scenic changes, storage, audience seating.
   Special visual effects (physical, video, lighting).
   Safety precautions, regulations, etc., involved.

Action: Director indicates possible performers' positions, action, business.

Cameras: Number of cameras; types of mountings; key positions for each scene. Probable camera moves.
   Any special camera accessories needed (eg: canted shots).
   Specialists estimate feasibility of anticipated treatment (re sufficient working space, time for moves, camera cable routing, etc.).

Lighting: Discussion of lighting treatment feasibility, relative to scenic design, action, sound pick-up, time/equipment/manpower availability. Discussion of pictorial effects, atmosphere, etc. Discussion of picture-matching to film or videotape.

Audio: Similar discussion to 'Lighting'. Discussion of audio pick-up methods, potential problems. Audio inserts considered (prerecorded, library sounds, spot effects, music).

Video Effects: Chroma-key (CSO), electronic treatment.

Artwork/Titling: Graphics, displays, etc.

Further Technical Facilities: Equipment organisation, re filming or pre-studio videotaping for production. Also technical resources required for studio production: telecine (film channel), videotape, video-disc, slide-scanner, picture monitors, prompters, cueing facilities required.

Scheduling: Pre-studio shooting. Filming, videotape, audio recording. Experimental sessions.
Pre-studio rehearsals. Read through, block action, dry run (technical run).
Studio rehearsal. Setting (staging) and lighting. Camera rehearsal times, and arrangements. Meal breaks. Technical periods (camera line-up). Recording periods. Editing periods and facilities.

Staging Plan

The *studio plan* (floor plan) is a standard scale drawing, showing the permanent studio staging area, together with studio features and facilities (exits, cyclorama, technical supplies, storage rooms, etc.). This tracing forms the basis of a series of derived plans. Its next step, the *staging (setting) plan,* shows all scenic arrangements (shape and positions of sets, main furnishing, set dressing). On this, the director plans his shots, and subsequently marks the main positions of cameras and sound booms (sometimes performers' positions). This becomes the *camera plan.* Using the camera plan, the lighting director devises a *lighting plot,* containing details of lamp-types and positions, supplies, etc., to be used in the lighting treatment.

Developing the staging plan
Although individuals have their own methods, let us examine a typical approach when developing the studio *staging plan (setting plan).*

Break the production down into its scenes or sequences. How many sets are needed? (Any multi-use or revamping?) Sketch plans of possible settings with necessary main features (doors, windows) on separate pieces of tracing paper. Check that each set is of appropriate size and scale for the scene. If it is too small, action and shot variety become limited. But for restricted action, even a single flat may suffice. Large settings only offer really good production value in long shots, and with widespread action (not in localised close shots). Place these set outlines on the studio plan in potential positions. Preferably, arrange the sets around the studio in shooting order, and avoid unnecessary equipment moves between sets. Adjust the position and shape of each set to allow easy access for cameras, sound boom, lighting treatment. An 'operational zone' in front of the set provides for equipment movement and positioning. Keep any camera moves within the average three-walled setting to a minimum. Allow room for performers to enter and leave sets, ie: offstage space behind doorways, access steps for parallels (stands). Allow floor space for temporary storage areas during production such as movable scenery, properties, standby items, graphics, title stands, monitors and loudspeakers. Consider studio access from nearby storage areas for technical equipment, and fire lane restrictions.

Finally, the director checks the potential camera viewpoints (movable flats or swingers, may be necessary). Possible shoot-off points are dealt with (possibly requiring masking, or wall extensions). The compositional value of scenic features is also considered. For instance, small features, such as windows, that appear in a number of shots from different viewpoints, tend to have compositional advantages over a single main feature that is mostly out of shot, or, conversely, dominates all shots. Also, excessive detail can clutter the shots.

100

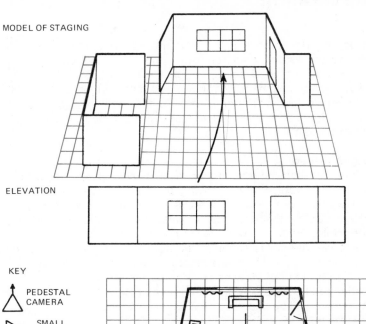

MODEL OF STAGING

ELEVATION

KEY

PEDESTAL
CAMERA

SMALL

SOUNDBOOMS

LARGE

FURNITURE

TABLES

CHAIR

ARMCHAIR

SETTEE
COUCH

TALENT

MOVEMENTS

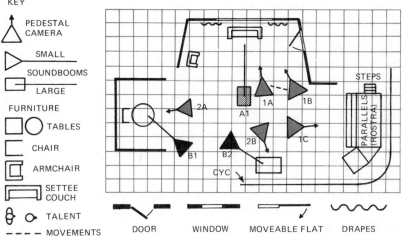

DOOR   WINDOW   MOVEABLE FLAT   DRAPES

THE STAGING PLAN

The staging model

The scale *model* is made in card from *elevations* of the setting stuck on a plan. It shows basic structural and surface details.

The camera plan

The staging plan shows the settings distributed around the setting area, together with their furniture. Cameras and sound-boom positions are indicated. (Booms: A1,B1,2. Cameras: 1A,B,C. 2A,B. 3A,B.)

101

Shot Planning

No director *creates* with a protractor and squared paper. He thinks in terms of *pictures* – of visual arrangements that produce a particular effect or mood. But good shots, coupled with smooth compositional continuity, do not just happen. They need forethought and planning. With experience, 'guesstimates' can be made. Real accuracy requires scale calculations. But they are a creative aid, not a substitute for imaginative thought.

Planning in private
Paper planning saves studio rehearsal time. Moreover, ideas can be worked out in private, without having to trundle pedestals around to see what will happen. The tools are a scale plan, and a transparent triangle representing the lens angle (an adjustable protractor is ideal).

The principles involved are quite simple. The angle at the apex of the transparent triangle is the same as the horizontal angle of the camera lens to be used (eg: 25°). Wherever it is placed on the studio plan, it shows the same field of view as covered by the studio camera with its lens positioned at the apex. When the angle does not fall within the set, then the camera will be shooting off if set up at that point in the studio.

Shot proportions
The lines that form the angle represent the left and right edges of the screen. If an object is positioned so that it touches both of the lines, it exactly fills the screen width – whether it is a small close object, or a large distant one.

Suppose an object is required to fill *a certain proportion of the screen width* (say, one third). Multiply the object's width by that proportion (eg: 3) and, taking a piece of paper of this marked length, move it until it fits then appear to fill one third of the shot width. Suppose the subject is a person (full face is $\frac{3}{4}$in wide on a $\frac{1}{4}$in. scale, for a person is roughly 18 inches across the shoulders*). To fill one third of the screen with a person full-faced, move a 3 $\times\frac{3}{4}$in. marker until it fills the angle. On a 25° lens, the measured result is $3\frac{1}{2}$ft. away.

Opposite is a quick shot check for a 25° lens. This shows all the subject distances at which the standard shots (page 31) can be obtained with a 25° lens. If you are using another lens angle, multiply the table distance by that factor:

$$50°=\tfrac{1}{2}. \ \ 10°=2\cdot5. \ \ 40°=\frac{25}{40} \ \text{(ie: }0\cdot6).$$

*Metric scale: People are roughly 0·45 metre across, 0·25 deep.

102

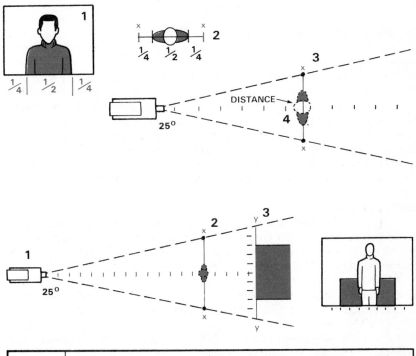

SHOT	BCU	CU HEAD/SHLDRS.	MCU CHEST	MID-SHOT WAIST	¾ SHOT KNEES	FULL LENGTH
FT.	3	4	5.5	7	14	+20
M.	0.86	1.27	1.72	2.10	4.26	+6.08

SHOT PLANNING

How can we get this shot?
Check your scale used. (If $\frac{1}{4}$in. = 1ft., a man is $\frac{3}{8}$in. across).   1. How much of shot does he occupy (eg $\frac{1}{2}$).   2. Draw scale line with man $\frac{1}{2}$ its length.   3. Fit line across lens angle (at X – X).   4. Read distance needed to get shot.

What does this set–up give?
Man is 14ft. away on 25° lens, therefore: This is a $\frac{3}{4}$-*shot (knee shot)* in table below. For any item, draw line across angle at that point (eg X – X). This shows shot width at that distance. What proportion of shot is occupied by desk? Desk is at Y – Y, 6 units wide. Shot width 10 units at that point, therefore desk fills $\frac{6}{10}$ = 0.6 of screen.

Scripting for TV

Scripting enables one to tailor the production predictably.

Scripting forms
TV scripting takes two basic forms. 'Preliminary scripting' is the more widely used method. Here a script is written before the production is rehearsed and recorded, and is modified only slightly, as circumstances require. 'Post scripting' is usually found where a precise story line and commentary can only be devised once the production has been edited into at least rough form (eg: compilation programmes from a series of existing shows, documentary programmes). A preliminary shot-list or draft script helps to provide a foundation for the final treatment.

Script style
The usual aim in writing the TV script, is to tell the story in visual terms, if possible. The accompanying sound extends its significance, explaining and augmenting what is seen. Where sound predominates the picture should still be meaningful (page 126). Avoid talks with slides.

The *style* of the script must always relate to the *spoken* word, not the written page. Remember, to write as if for an individual viewer or a small group not a public meeting. Over-complicated ideas obscure thought. Use simple words and short sentences. The type of audience and the time available determine the way ideas should be developed, how much can be said, and the elaboration and depth called for.

Getting the ideas across
The more complex the subject, the easier should be the stages of explanation. Always bear in mind the *assimilation rate* – the time it takes to see, recognise and understand the significance of each point. It varies according to the familiarity or otherwise of facts to the viewer. A sequence of fresh, difficult information may need an introduction and a summary. Avoid giving too many facts too quickly, but make one point at a time. Where several activities are shown simultaneously, the audience becomes confused. Development should be gradual and progressive, avoiding returning to or repeating points unnecessarily.

Script mechanics
The script has to be technically possible with the budget, facilities, skills available. It needs to allow for studio mechanics (eg: time to move cameras, or alter a caption title). With commentary to film or videotape include pauses, so that there is no danger of it getting out of step with the most important shots if the commentator speeds or slows his delivery a little. It is better for the explanation to precede the picture slightly, rather than lag while the viewer wonders what it is about.

SHOT	CAM. (POSITION)	SCENE	INT./EXTR.	LOCATION	TIME OF DAY

CAMS. 1B, 2D, 3C. SOUND BOOMS A3, B4.

3. INT. KITCHEN DAY

20. 2 D

BCU PAT'S hands,
showing counting
coins.
PULL BACK SLOWLY,
to CU stopping at
door knock.

(PAT IS SEATED AT
TABLE, A BOX BEFORE HIM,
FROM WHICH HE TAKES GOLD
COINS. HE COUNTS AND
PILES THEM. THERE IS A
KNOCK AT THE DOOR.)

PAT: What do you want? (INCOHERENT
SOUND FROM OUTSIDE DOOR)

21. 1 B

BCU Door latch
ZOOM OUT to MS as
door opens.

Who's there, I say! /
(THUMPING ON DOOR.
DOOR LATCH RISES. A
BODY FALLS IN, ONTO
THE FLOOR.)

22. 3 C

MCS of MIKE
sprawled on floor.

What in the name of ..... /

23. 2 D

2s HOLD PAT as
he comes round
table.

MIKE: It's me. I've got to see you. /

PAT: What's wrong with you man?
Are you drunk or something?   /

24. 1 B

CU Back of MIKE'S
head. We see he
is injured. He
looks up to PAT.
TILT UP to MCU PAT
(POV shot)

PAT: Don't lie there. Get up and
tell me what you want.

25. 3 C

MLS PAT.
MIKE staggers
to his feet.

Is there something ailing you? /

MIKE: They're out in the woods.
Can't you hear them?
One of them hit me. /

26. 2 D

ARC LEFT as PAT
grabs MIKE'S arm
and seats him
in chair.

PAT: Are you badly hurt?
You look awful!

Too much stultifies action. Too little allows unreliability.

Production Paperwork

Most creative workers hate paperwork. It is time-consuming to prepare. We doubt its accuracy after changes have been introduced. It can be confining and restricting to freedom of thought.

In reality, paperwork is an unavoidable link in providing dependable, complete facilities and operation and in ensuring coherent, unified teamwork. The larger the organisation, the greater the need. Production paperwork takes so many forms (literally!) ranging from contracts, requisitions, permits, expenses, etc., to those directly guiding the studio team. Each specialist job has its spurious associated documents, to arrange facilities, materials, labour, transport. Some may be used to feed computers, some just to remind Joe of a 'phone call. But certain types of production paperwork are universal to all TV studio organisation.

Scripts
The corrected draft script gives the story line/synopsis, dialogue, narration, basic scene-setting, action outline and stage directions. After working over, it becomes the *rehearsal script*. Here the page is split vertically. The existing script material is contained in the right-hand half, which is primarily concerned with audio information. As the director develops his picture treatment, this new camera information is typed in the blank left-hand section of the page. The combined script, now complete with all the production details the team needs to coordinate its shots, moves, cueing, timing, etc., has become the *camera script*.

A *semi-scripted* show usually follows a much simpler format. Basic camera shots are indicated, with anticipated action, any agreed dialogue such as introductory or concluding speech, with indications of questions, graphics inserts, etc.

Running order/show format
This list segments the production, showing the programme items, the set areas (scenes) involved, video and audio facilities needed (lighting conditions), major running time, and intended segment durations, together with performers' names.

Camera cards/shot sheets/crib cards/shot list
The busy cameraman is too preoccupied to read a script. Instead, he has a series of cards clipped to his camera, giving him details for each of his shots. This includes the shot number, floor position (as marked on the camera plan), sometimes the lens angle, and a description of the shot (people involved, and their action) and camera movements, together with any additional instructions (eg: 'Hold 2-shot as they go to the door'). It may contain too, a rough sketch of the studio layout, showing respective positions of the cameras (1A, 1B, 1C, etc.).

RUNNING ORDER

Page	Scene	Shots	Cams/Booms		D/N	Cast
1	1. INT. WOODSHED	1 - 9	1A, 3A,	A1	DAY	Mike Jane
3	EXT. WOODSHED	10 - 12	2A,	F/P	DAY	Jane Jim
	RECORDING BREAK					
4	2. INT. SHOP	13 - 14	4A,	B1	DAY	George
6	3. EXT. WOODS	15	1B, 3B,	A2	DAY	Mike George
7	4. INT. SHOP	16 - 20	4A,	B1	DAY	George

CAMERA CARD

CAMERA ONE   THE OLD MILL HOUSE   STUDIO B

SHOT	POSN.	LENS ANGLE*	SET
2	A	24°	1. WOODSHED LS TABLE PAN MIKE L. to window.
5	(A)	35°	MS MIKE moves R. to stove JANE into shot L. Hold 2-shot as they X to wood-pile.

MOVE TO POSITION 'B' during Shot 6.

21	B	10°	BCU Door latch. ZOOM OUT to MS as door opens.
24	(B)	24°	CU back MIKE'S head. As he looks up, TILT UP to MCU of PAT (POV shot)

* OPTIONAL

Pre-studio Rehearsal

If a show has a *static* format (interviews, talks, quizzes, panels), rehearsal preliminaries may simply consist of the director discussing the production with the performers, so that they know what is expected of them. But where the production is mobile, complex, and contains interrelated action, where performance and timing are tightly controlled, pre-rehearsal before camera time is essential.

Preliminaries
It is self-evident that for any *dramatic* production, we need to arrange and practise the various moves, business, lines, etc., until all concerned have achieved interrelated performances. Rehearsals begin with a *briefing, read through* or *line rehearsal,* in which the director outlines his interpretation of the work, and the cast becomes familiar with reading lines together, and the required characterisations.

The equivalent stage for a *demonstration* programme, would be discussion and organisation of the programme format, the range and depth of the items and methods of presenting and demonstrating facts.

Pre-rehearsal/outside rehearsal
Studio time and space are usually at a premium. So, although it would be an advantage to be able to rehearse the entire show 'for real' in the setting to be used, this is generally impracticable. Instead, the performers have to be content with rehearsal under 'mock-up' conditions, in a convenient rehearsal hall or hired room.

Here the floor is taped or chalked with a full-size plan layout of the studio setting. Doors, windows, stairways, etc., are outlined. Stock rehearsal furniture substitutes the actual items used in the studio, and major props such as a hatstand, phone or tableware are provided. The cast soon become accustomed to the scale and features of their surroundings, particularly where vertical poles, chairs or dummy doors, mark the main architectural features.

The director arranges the positions, grouping, action, to suit the production treatment he has in mind. He rehearses the production in sections: the cast, learning their lines, practising their performances, moves and business, until the entire work runs smoothly, ready for its studio debut. The director scrutinises rehearsals, standing in turn at his various planned camera positions, checking shots through his viewfinder, adjusting details as necessary.

Finally, a few days before the production is due in the studio, the specialists who were at the production planning meeting watch a *technical run-through,* checking and anticipating problems for cameras, lighting, sound, etc. This is the version from which the lighting plot and facilities are finalised

Pre-studio rehearsal hints – initial blocking

The preliminary read-through will only give the roughest estimate of timing. But, after allowances have been made for typical business, action, recorded inserts, etc., a probable duration should emerge. Anticipate potential script cuts if overrun is evident.

Ensure as early as possible that the performers have a clear idea of the programme format, their part in it, and perhaps their interrelationship with others' contributions.

Make sure that performers have a good notion of the setting (using sketches, models, plans), what it represents, where things are in it. Provide reasonable substitutes, where real props are not available. Where specific apparatus is involved, only the actual item to be used in the studio may suffice. (Where unfamiliar attire is eventually to be worn – eg: sword, hoop-skirt, cloak – a rehearsal version is preferable to dummy motions).

Maintain a firm attitude towards punctuality, inattention, background chatter during rehearsals, to avoid needless time wastage and frustrations.

Be careful that actors' positions are consistent, meaningful (ie: they do not stand 'on' a wall), or shot arrangements become meaningless.

Use a portable viewfinder to arrange shots. Even a card cut-out frame or a hand-formed frame is better than unaided guesses.

Avoid excessive revisions of action, grouping, line-cuts, etc. Wrong versions get remembered, new ones forgotten.

Always think in terms of *shots,* not of theatrical-styled groupings, entrances, exits, business. Start with clear ideas *at script stage* about what you want the camera to show, rather than arrange 'nice groups' and try to get 'good shots' during rehearsal.

There is a tendency when setting up shots in a rehearsal hall, to overlook the scenic background that will actually be present in the studio. Check shots with the set designer's plans and elevations.

Performers should have a good idea of the shots you are taking – whether, for instance, they are in a revealing close-up, where even slight movement counts, or whether they are out of picture.

Particularly when taking close shots, always consider depth-of-field limitations. Deep shots (with close and distant people framed together) may not be sharp overall on camera.

Think in terms of practical studio mechanics. Rapid repositioning while looking through a viewfinder may be physically impossible with an actual camera.

Try to bear audio and lighting problems in mind when arranging action and positions. For example, where individuals spaced widely apart talk consecutively, the sound boom may need time to swing, or have to be supplemented.

The pipe dreams come to life.

Studio Rehearsals

The studio floor is a hive of activity as the director arrives for his final pre-rehearsal check-over.

Rehearsal begins – blocking
Some directors begin studio rehearsal with a *dry run (walkthrough)*, in which the studio crew watch a performance (without cameras) as they learn of the production format and treatment. (Remember, only key members of the team have attended planning and rehearsals.)

For most directors, though, rehearsals begin with *camera blocking (first run, stopping run, stagger through)*. A few prefer to work beside a mobile picture monitor on the studio floor, calling shots, checking and altering where necessary, until each section is complete. They then watch it as a continuous run, from the production control room. Most directors, however, control operations throughout from the control room, only 'going to the floor' (ie: the studio action area) when personal, on-the-spot discussion is unavoidable. Otherwise, all communication to the crew is through the communal intercom system, while instructions to the talent pass through the floor manager.

In the production control room, the director maintains a watchful eye on the *master (line) monitor,* while preparing the shots he is seeing on *preview (channel)* monitors. During this visual agility, he concurrently assesses his production, guides cameras into the shots he is seeking, sorts out snags and snarl-ups and works out substitute treatment where necessary. Of course, he is also judging performances, evaluating the various contributory factors to his show, and considering what improvements would be practicable. He also cues all action (to start and stop), and either makes or cues all picture transitions. The director's assistant continually notes timings and durations, and warns various contributory sources (eg: film channel) to stand-by as their cueing point approaches. (The Producer, whose principal role has been to set up and mastermind the business and economic aspects of the production, may provide the director with critical comment and advice.)

Some directors rehearse and correct a scene or section at a time; while others cover an entire sequence or an act before correcting. Some prefer a *stop-start* method, picking up again before each error point. Others aim at a run that is as uninterrupted as possible.

Final stages
A *continuous run-through* is a 'polishing' rehearsal, giving a better idea of shot effectiveness, continuity, pace, timing, operational problems, etc. Only when it is unavoidable does one stop to remedy shortcomings. But the *dress-run* aims at an on-air performance, without any unscheduled stops, or errors.

110

Effective Studio Rehearsal

Examine each shot. Modify it if necessary to improve positions, action, movement, composition.

Consider *shot continuity.* Alterations may affect earlier shots, too.

Remember, the crew and performers are *memorising.* Their aids are the paperwork (script, camera cards, cue sheets) and your intercom reminders/instructions.

Don't be vague. Make sure that everyone knows what you are seeking to do. Do not try to correct errors by unexplained instructions (eg: 'Move it left a bit'). Indicate briefly *why* a shot is not working. Explain what it should be.

Avoid too many changes and revisions or there will be hesitations and mistakes.

Even in the first rehearsal, important *operational and performance errors,* misjudgments, inaccuracies, should be checked directly they occur (eg: camera in shot, shooting off, late cue, wrong lines, wrong shot, wrong mike). But avoid an over-interrupted rehearsal, or there will be poor continuity between shots.

If a cameraman offers alternative shots, for example to overcome a problem, indicate if you accept it or disagree, and why.

At the end of each scene or sequence, ask if there are any problems, and whether anyone wants to do that section again (cameras chalk their positions on floor).

Various staging and lighting defects are unavoidable in early rehearsal. Certain details (set-dressing, light effects) take time to complete. Some aspects need to be seen on camera before they can be corrected, such as overbright lights or lens flares. Shot readjustments during camera rehearsal often necessitate lighting alterations.

Never repeat a section (in rehearsal or recording), without saying whether it is to be *changed* (eg: move faster next time), or is to correct an *error* (eg: late cue), or to *polish* the performance/operations and let it flow more smoothly.

Ensure that everyone knows when shots have been deleted, or new shots added (ie: Shot 2A, 2B, 2C).

At the end of each rehearsal, check timings, give notes to performers/cast and crew, on any errors to be corrected, changes needed, problems to be solved. Check whether they have difficulties that need your aid.

At least one complete, uninterrupted rehearsal is essential for reliable transmission.

Rehearsal Problems – and Solutions

Even the best-planned production has its odd problems – but simple solutions are usually possible. Here are summaries of regular situations to look out for.

Getting the shot right

Subject detail not sufficiently visible: Move subject or camera closer, zoom in; explore subject with camera; use sectionalised shots (inserts, split-screen, page 144); do not attempt very close shots where detail is unsharp such as in a newspaper illustration. Obscured? Defocused? Shadowed? Stop and rectify.

Extreme close-ups of details required, but problems arise, due to limited focused depth, unsteady handling, moving in/out of frame: Place item on pre-marked position on firm surface. Light specially; stop lens down. (Wide-angle lenses distort perspective badly and need to be closer to item.) Use photo-caption of detail.

Subject's shape does not fit 4 by 3 TV screen (for instance, a tall, or round item): Take long shot of whole item (detail will now be small), and show features by panning/tilting, or intercutting closer shots. When problem is due to items being spaced widely apart, recompose shot (move them together, arrange them in depth in picture, or shoot diagonally). (Pages 83, 147.)

Bad framing. Subject unattractively cut off by edge of shot. Too little or too much space around subject: adjust shot and recompose. Subject too high (or low) in frame: adjust headroom.

One subject masks (obscures) another: Relocate and floor-mark new positions. Check any previous shots from other viewpoints, with new subject positions.

Subjects appear too spaced apart in shot: Move them closer together, shoot obliquely, or intercut single shots.

Subject too large (or small) relative to others in shot: Change subject/camera distance for main subject, perhaps altering lens angle too (wider angle exaggerates size differences with distance).

Subject appears too prominent (reduce the shot size) or too important (increase camera height).

Background objects or scenic lines seen 'growing out of' foreground subject: Move, cover-up or remove background item; reposition camera or subject; reduce prominence of background (defocus; less light).

Unwanted distortion of subject. Misshapen due to close wide-angle lens; or depth squashed, flattened ('cardboarded') as lens angle too narrow: alter lens angle and camera distance accordingly.

Check monochrome picture: Ensure that it is effective rendering of colour shot.

Performers

Out of position (off marks): Correct and give toe marks or location points.

Facing wrong camera: Inform; drawing attention to camera tally (cue) light illuminated when camera selected.

Inaccurate dialogue (cuts out lines, dries/fluffs, or freezes, and needs prompt, wrong lines): Use prompter, cue cards, concealed notes, verbal prompts (with audio 'cut key').

Untidy appearance (hair, tie, collar askew): Diplomatic neatening!

Scenic

Check for overbright, distracting features: Repaint, remove, cover over, gauze cover, relight, re-angle, use dulling spray.

Colours or tones unsuitable (eg: subject merges into background): Adjust, replace, relight.

Check for background blemishes (dirty marks, tears, scrapes, wrinkles, etc.): Rectify, refurbish, cover over, relight.

Ugly or distracting shadows on background: Performers or scenery too close to background? Lighting angle too shallow?

Operational

Camera shooting off set: Alter shot, extend background scenery, or add foreground masking.

Lens flares or other spurious light images: Raise camera viewpoint, improve lens hood (shade), shield off or heighten lighting. Revise shot.

Unwanted/extraneous subjects in shot: Check if their positions have altered since last rehearsal. Remove unwanted items. Tighten shot to exclude. Rearrange shot.

Boom microphone in shot: Check with audio personnel. Avoid cutting from close to distant shots on same speaker. Warn boom operator before cutting. Recompose shot. Alter sound pick-up method.

Boom shadows on people or background: Check with audio/lighting personnel if avoidable. Consider modifying shot, using a shot tighter, or altered viewpoint. Alter sound pick-up or lighting.

Any cables in shot? (Audio, lighting, monitor, camera cables): Remove from shot.

Captions/graphics/titling. Is it straight and level? Can it all be seen and read (sufficiently large, sufficient time)?

Editing/Video Switching/Vision Mixing

Any distractions on cutting? Avoid reverse cuts, jump cuts, jumps in position, size or frame height. Any loss of direction or location?

Any distractions on mixing (dissolve)? Avoid image confusion during long mix.

The director's alter ego.

Floor Manager

The floor manager (FM) is the director's contact man on the studio floor. As well as conveying the director's instructions to the performers, he covers local liaison, checks organisation, and ensures the smooth running of studio activities. He may meet the director just as the production reaches the studio, or may have helped earlier in its preparation (planning, pre-rehearsals, filming) aided by his assistant (AFM).

Rehearsal preparations
While pre-rehearsal preparations take place (dressing sets, setting lights, positioning equipment, etc.), the FM checks all non-technical aspects of the production – that everyone is ready to rehearse on time, any hitches with scenery, furniture, that action props and scenery work (eg: cigarette lighters, room doors, etc.), that the graphics, models, demonstration apparatus etc. are present, and fire and safety regulations are complied with. He also checks that performers have arrived, been accommodated, and know when they're wanted and that any visitors or photo-calls, are likely.
The director's assistant gives out scripts, camera cards, slides, etc., and checks accuracy of titling (cast lists, etc.).

Rehearsal duties
During rehearsal, the FM wears earphones ('cans', 'deaf-aid' earpiece) attached either to a miniature radio receiver, or a long lead plugged to the general production talkback circuit. He and the studio crew (cameras, audio, prompters, etc.) receive instructions and information, unheard by the studio mikes or the performers.

The FM cues and guides performers, smoothing their difficulties and diplomatically relaying the director's messages. Only the FM will normally stop rehearsal (on the director's behalf), anticipating problems, rearranging action or grouping, improving furniture positions, etc. While maintaining general studio discipline, the FM investigates and aims to clear any delays, suggesting alternative sections to rehearse during delays.The FM speaks to the director over the studio mikes, or a reverse talkback circuit. Often, a gesture in front of a camera suffices. He may explain or correct problems not seen by the director. Cameras can turn and show obstacles, foot positions, etc.

The FM announces all studio breaks, and recommencing times, ensures that all is ready for rehearsals and recording, a smooth 'turn round' to opening positions after each rehearsal. At recording time, he readies the studio, and counts down to the start. At its end, he holds the studio while the videotape is checked, then announces and prepares for retakes. Finally, he releases the studio, checks out any special items, and logs his report.

FLOOR MANAGER SIGNALS

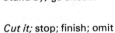

Stand by; go ahead.

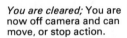

Cut it; stop; finish; omit rest of item.

You are cleared; You are now off camera and can move, or stop action.

Volume up; louder.

Volume down; quiter (sometimes precede by "Quiet" signal).

Quiet; stop applause.

Tighten-up; Get closer together.

Open-up; Move further apart.

Come nearer; come downstage.

Go further away; go upstage.

You're on that camera, play to that camera; (Sometimes preceded by "Turning actor's head" gesture.)

Play to the light indicated; (When actors are shadowing, point to light source and to area of face shadowed.)

Turn around (in direction indicated).

Speed up; faster pace; quicker tempo. (Movement's speed shows amount of increase).

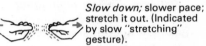

Slow down; slower pace; stretch it out. (Indicated by slow "stretching" gesture).

O.K.; you're all right now; it's O.K. (Confirmation signal.)

We're/you're on time.

Are we on time? How is time going?

You have . . . time left (Illustrated—2 mins. and ½ min).

Wind-up now.

To audience; *you can applaud now.* (May be followed by "Louder" signal).

Stop; (For applause, widespread action, etc.).

115

Learn effective intercom techniques.

Guiding the Crew

Remote from the studio, the director must convey his ideas quickly and precisely.

Intercom
How detailed intercom instructions need to be depends on crew experience, and the show's complexity. Intercom should provide a balanced flow of information, avoiding continuous chat and random gossip. A *cut-key* switches the circuit off when necessary.

Attitude to the crew
The inexperienced director frequently has the urge to dash down to the studio floor to explain directly what he wants to do. Good TV direction does not work that way. It wastes rehearsal time, and while it helps individuals such as a cameraman, it often leaves others uninformed of changes now necessary (lighting or sound). The director must have a clear idea of what he wants. The crew may know little or nothing of his intentions, and they have relatively little time to find out what is expected of them, and to practise and coordinate their respective contributions.

Be patient! The dictatorial director is a pain in the neck – especially when he is wrong! But the undecided bumblings of the director who has not thought out his show, and relies on the crew to carry him, is no better. If an operation is not right, or has not been understood, find out if there is a problem. Each camera has reverse-talkback (private wire or line, camera talkback), either as an individual circuit, or, more often, via the communal system.* Listen to suggestions, and accept or reject them in firm, but friendly terms.

Always help the crew by warning them of action, particularly in early rehearsals. A quick guide, such as 'He's going to get up here' (prepare for a rise), smooths operations considerably. Let everyone know immediately about any extra shots or cuts.

General points
The preview monitors are your eyes. Watching them carefully, you can anticipate trouble, seeing that a boom will be in shot when you cut, that a shot is wrong. Corrections made on preview will prevent errors being seen on the transmission (main) channel.

End-of-rehearsal notes are either *instructive,* such as 'Zoom in faster on Shot 9', or *suggestions* like 'Will it help Camera 2 on Shot 25 if the girl pauses before moving?'. Make it clear when a rehearsal or taping session is over, and retakes complete. Never fail to thank the crew – particularly individuals who have done outstanding work.

*Party line (US); studio talkback; general talkback (Brit).

Typical Shot Calls by the Director's Assistant

During rehearsal and transmission, the director's assistant continually passes information over the talkback, to guide continuity, prepare sources, and aid timing. Let us 'listen' to part of a typical, well-organised production.

CALLS	MEANING
On Shot 291 . . . 2 next	Shot 291 is 'on the air'. Stand by Camera 2.
Stand by film (or TK, ie telecine)	Preparing film channel for cue.
Shot 292 . . . 3 next	
On 3 . . . Film (or TK) next	On Camera 3. Film ready for cue.
Run film (or TK) . . . Counting down, 8–7–6–5–4–3–2–1–zero	Start cue to film, film-leader running, counting down to start.
On film for 3 minutes, 17 seconds	
One minute left on film. Out words ' . . . and so to bed'.	End warning for film. Stand by for next shot.
Coming to Shot 293, on Cam. 3.	
30 seconds . . . 20–10–5–4–3–2–1–0	Counting back to the studio.
Shot 293 on 3	On Camera 3.
Shots 294, 295 are *cut*	Warning reminder of shots cut from scripted version.
Next is 296 on 1 . . . steady 1	Stand by Cam. 1 (was not steady on his shot).
Shot 296 on 1 . . . 3 next	On Cam. 1. Stand by Cam. 3.
Extra shots 297 A and B	Warning reminder of shots added to scripted version.
Shot 297 on 3 . . . 297A on 2 next.	On Cam. 3. Stand by Cam. 2.
Shot 297A on 2 . . . Clear 1 to roller.	Cam. 2. Cam. 1 to move to title roller (crawl titles, roller caption).
Next 297B on 3	Stand by Cam. 3.
Shot 297B on 3. Stand by music and roller.	On Cam. 3. Stand by to audio tape and end titles.
Go music. Go roller.	Cue to start audio taped music, and operate rolling end titles shot on Cam. 1.
Stand by for retakes	Studio held while sections requiring re-recording selected.
We have a clear.	Videorecording checked and OK.

Guiding the Performers

How much guidance performers need depends on such factors as their experience, whether the show is scripted, with learned lines or a prompter, and the complexity of action – moves, performance.

Inexperienced talent
We may need to do little more than receive the talent, make him feel at ease, and outline what we want him to do. Do not expect too much of an inexperienced performer. Keep his problems to a minimum, supporting him if possible with an experienced host/anchorman. He needs reassurance and confidence, to do his best.

Do not overburden him with instructions. When necessary, explain how to show items to the camera, and hold them still for close-ups. Avoid elaborate action or moves, and do not rearrange and alter these if possible. It creates confusion. You may need to tell him whether he is to address the camera (and which one), or the host. If he must move around, indicate the positions required. Check that he understands.

Quite small things such as movements around the camera can distract or worry a performer. Confidence may be strengthened by allowing a person to have a small cue card, or a list of points beside the camera. But inexperienced people do not read scripts or prompters 'naturally', and have a stilted, ill-at-ease delivery.

Where a person lacking TV experience is demonstrating a piece of equipment or apparatus, we can often achieve a more spontaneous, predictable performance by having him show his material to an experienced host/anchorman, who can guide him by questions, and ensure that articles are positioned for the camera.

Professional talent
The professional performer in a non-drama production is familiar with studio routine, can take the FM's instructions from the corner of an eye, keeps cool under the most trying conditions, and remains in command of the situation whatever happens around him. He may wear an earpiece relaying switched studio talkback (operated when the director throws a key), over which he hears comments, suggestions, timings or changes of plan without an eyebrow's twitch although on camera!

Try to avoid the uncertainties of under-rehearsal, or the tedium of over-rehearsal. Avoid inaction, and the fall-off in interest that comes from waiting around. If you have to wait for someone or something to arrive, see if there is anything that can be rehearsed meanwhile. Otherwise, have a definite stand-down, with a specified return time.

It is always preferable for performers to run through their material before recording time – even with substitute questions or discussion. However, if performers are not available until on-air time, use stand-ins to line-up shots and rehearse, rather than rely on hopeful inspiration.

Watching monitors
A nearby monitor can be a strong temptation for a person to watch himself!

Toe marks
Chalk or crayon marks around feet, show talent their rehearsed position when there are no locating points.

Locating points
A person may be located by a piece of furniture – to ensure accurate positioning of shots.
Within a setting, they may use various scenic features as locating points as they move around.

119

Cueing

A cue is given to start or to stop action – to indicate when to speak, move, operate equipment, and so on. This requires careful timing, anticipating the exact moment, and how long the recipient will take to respond. Action and dialogue which is cued too *early* begins before it is switched. With *late* cueing, there is a cut to a shot, in which action springs into life as we watch. Wrong cueing leaves performers on the screen bewildered after they have finished their contribution and unsure whether to ad lib or just grin. Film or videotape inserts run out. We may even see a film-leader running-up (counting down).

Forms of cueing
Word cues are agreed 'go-ahead' points during dialogue, commentary, or discussion, to cue action (a move, or an entrance), or to switch to an insert. *Out cues* or *out words* (pages 117, 124), are the word cues at the end of a filmed or taped insert.

Hand cues given by the FM are a standard method of starting studio action (page 115). Where the talent cannot see the FM, the cue may be relayed – occasionally a tap on the foot or shoulder may be necessary.

Monitor cues are taken from watching action on a studio monitor, and beginning commentary or action at an agreed point (eg: as a car door closes). A few seconds *run-in* and *run-out* picture (without dialogue) is used as a *cushion (buffer)* at the 'top' and 'tail' of any film or VTR insert. A *time-cue* is a countdown from a cue-point, before commentary or action begins.

Light cues may be taken from the *camera tally (cue) light,* which comes on as the camera is selected. Small portable *cue lights* can be used (for announce booths, or actors waiting behind scenery). The standby 'flick', followed by a steady 'action light'.

Buzzer cues are used in some areas (film or videotape to production control room). E.q. one buzz 'Yes' or 'Start'. Two buzzes 'No' or 'Stop'.

Talkback cues are given direct to a performer such as a newscaster, sports commentator wearing an earpiece.

Clock cues are go-aheads at a specific time.

Electronic cue-dots appear as small black/white squares or circles in the corner of the transmitted picture at network programme-change points say 30 to 10 sec. and 5 to 0 sec.

Film cueing
Film is set up in the projector (telecine) at a chosen cue-marked point. On starting the machine, the first required picture frame then appears after a known delay, eg: 4 secs. So if the machine is started about 12 words before the switching point, studio dialogue will stop just as the 'in-frame' appears. The cue-mark may be a sync-numeral on a standard film leader (eg: 4) or a marked frame. (An 8 sec. 25 word cue may be used).

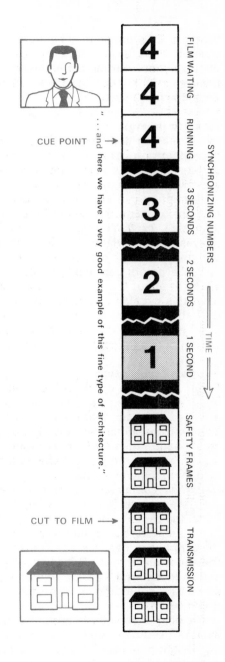

The principles of film cueing
The film is laced up, projecting the chosen synchronizing number. (this represents a known run-up time.)
At the cue point in the speech, 4 sec. before it is due to finish, the projector is started.
The film machine runs up to speed. Precisely 4 sec. later, the film pictures begin.
Safety (Buffer) frames allow for slight timing leeway.
As the speech ends we cut to the film, and its picture is transmitted instead.

121

Skilfully done, the audience remains unaware.

Prompting

Where a TV production is being recorded, there is the option of either treating it as a live performance and prompting performers when necessary, or inserting corrected *retake* sections in subsequent editing. If a live performance goes astray, we have no alternative than to prompt and hope for the best!

Need to prompt
Script reading does not make good television. Not only is it often inappropriate on camera, but there are always the problems of finding and keeping one's place, and avoiding a dull reading voice that lacks spontaneity. Even the experienced can get too reliant on their scripts.

Prompting can have several purposes. It can be used as correction, to help the performer when he *dries* ('freezes' or stops, with 'instant amnesia'), or *fluffs* (makes an error, uses wrong dialogue), or *cuts* (leaves out material). A quiet aural cue from the FM may be possible perhaps pressing a *prompt button* to kill the mike temporarily.

While actors can learn scripts so that they are word-perfect, and speak at about the same rate for each rehearsal, relatively few others have this capability, and at best, some sort of *aide-memoire* is often desirable. This can range from a series of *subject-headings,* as 'just-in-case' reminders, or continual references, to large displays that present the entire text for continuous reading.

Types of prompters
Script boards are often used by commentators/anchormen/presenters/ interviewers. Their various notes, questions and research work, are attached to a clip board, and form the reference point for their work. Some professionals feel that this approach is too formal, and prefer small, hand-notes *(crib cards* around postcard size) or palmed notes. Actors have written a few strategic notes on scenery, before now, to help them remember lines.
Hand-held cards near the camera *(cue card, goof sheet, idiot card)* have their uses, as do *flipper cards* (flip cards) suspended in ring file fashion under the camera lens. *Earpieces* are really only for the experienced.
Roller prompters as a means of providing a continuously rolling copy of the script at or near the camera lens, are now very well established as the backbone of many TV shows. Designs vary (TelePrompter, Telesync, and Autocue are typical), the remotely-controlled, vari-speed roller presents type around $\frac{5}{8}$in. (15mm) high, with some 20 words visible in an 8-line frame.

Reading techniques ('casual' head movements) are necessary to avoid a fixed stare and to disguise eye movements. Reading distance and height may need to be adjusted to enable the talent to read easily, or prevent them from having to look into lights.

122

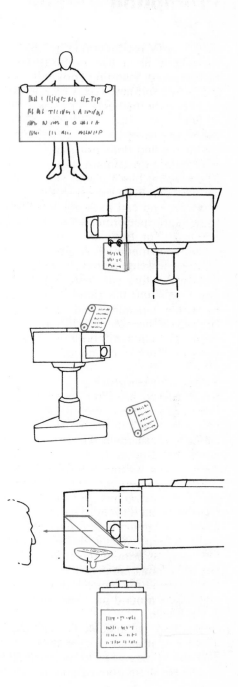

Hand-held card
A simple script, reminders, or messages can be written on a held-up card.

Flip cards
A series of flip cards hung on clips under the camera lens can summarise points for a speaker.

Roller sheet prompter
A continuously moving roller contains the script in 'jumbo' type. Its speed is adjustable by the speaker, or an operator.

Video prompter
An image of the script is displayed on a special TV picture tube within the prompter device. It is reflected towards the speaker by a glass sheet. He sees his lines as a moving text in front of the lens. The camera, shooting through the glass, sees only the speaker.

Production Timing

While a *closed-circuit* programme needs only approximate timing, a *live production* fitting into a time-slot, must often be accurate to a few seconds. Over-runs can result in the end of the show being cut off (eg: by commercial breaks), or cause scheduling problems. Inaccurate timing can completely abort any *composite production* in which various contributors 'opt-in' or 'opt-out' (temporarily join and leave) the main presentation, to insert their own material — eg: weather, or news items.

Live productions

Videotape can always be edited to a suitable length, but 'live' or 'live-on-tape' presentations lack this flexibility. Time must be watched continually. In an unscripted discussion, an early subject could easily outstay its welcome, so that an important later one had to be curtailed owing to time shortage.

To ensure controlled timing, a good chairman/anchorman continually evaluates, the situation, to ensure that agreed subjects are covered in allocated time periods. Where an item 'spreads' but is proving particularly productive, an editorial decision may deliberately restrict or drop others. If, despite careful timing, an item cannot be rounded off in the time. available, it is often better to indicate that with an apology, rather than struggle to complete it.

Hints on timing

Scripts can be roughly timed by reading them aloud, and allowing for mute action, business or inserts. Many scripts run for around a minute a page. At any pre-studio rehearsal, time scene-by-scene, or section-by-section. Devise a *timed running order* showing the duration of each item (estimated, permitted, or actual), and indicate where adjustments are desirable.

Although live sequences can inadvertently run short (speed up) or spread, pre-recorded *inserts* are always of a known duration. Recorded sections offer little time-flexibility (particularly when accompanied by a recorded commentary or dialogue), and can only be shortened — if at all — during transmission, by omitting the start or end.

Check all *recorded inserts* for their exact duration, and note their *out cues* (last words required). When cueing into the middle of material (eg: excerpt from a speech) *in cues* may be needed, ie: the first words to be heard. Wherever possible, the tops and tails of inserts should contain no speech or strong action (page 120).

To ensure that recorded music ends precisely at programme fade-out, time the music beforehand from a recognisable script point to its conclusion, eg: 2 mins. 25 secs. On transmission, start the music (faded down) 2 mins. 25 secs. before *programme out-time,* and fade it in when convenient.

Methods of Timing
Different methods of timing can be adopted according to the demands of the occasion.

Rehearsal timing
When rehearsal is halted for any reason, note the stop-watch time at that moment. When rehearsal recommences, go back to a point *before* the fault point. Continue the overall duration check when the *fault-point* is reached.

Forward timing (front timing)
Duration timing (estimated and real) as the show proceeds.

Items (desired durations)	Running Stop Watch reads (from prog. start)	Clock Start Time	Clock End Time	Item Running Times (Actual duration)
Introduction 30″	30″	19.15,00	19.15.30	30″
Item A 10′	10′30″	19.15.30	19.25.30	10′
Item B 8′	18′30″	19.25.30	19.33.30	8′

Back timing
A *'remaining time'* measurement, showing the amount of time before the programme ends.

Item Duration	Clock Time (Item Starts)	Remaining Time
1′	20.23.00	2′0″
Item Y 30″	20.24.00	1′0″
Item Z 30″	20.24.30	0·30″
End Titles Out Time	20.25.00	0·00″

Visual Padding

Although we may very occasionally dispense with sound, we can virtually never present the audience with a blank screen. Yet many subjects do not really have a strong *visual* element. It is very arguable how far reading, discussion, musical performances, for instance, really gain from our watching people *perform*. Some viewers like to see speakers' expressions, instrument fingering, etc., but this has really nothing to do with the intrinsic material or its *purpose* (ie: the argument, message, or the music itself). The attendant images are just as likely to distract us.

In certain types of programme situation, pictorial opportunities are far from obvious. We often cannot shoot an 'appropriate' subject because visuals do not exist, or it would be too costly to do so! Instead, we have to substitute *visual padding* that appears to be relevant.

The problem

Typical examples of occasions where there is a need to devise visual padding, include: *imaginary events* (hypothetical, fantasy); or *historical events* (before photography existed); or *concluded events* (the event is all over, and no traces remain); or cases where the camera *cannot shoot the subject* (it is inaccessible, or filming is not permitted); or it is *impracticable to shoot* (ie: meaningful shots cannot be obtained due to confined space, or it is too dangerous). Finally, there are occasions where a subject being discussed is *visually non-specific* (eg: 'Mankind'), or *abstract* (eg: 'Beauty'), or philosophical, so that there is no truly apposite matter for the camera to shoot.

Solutions to the problem

Talking heads are economical, but seldom compulsive viewing! We may be able to show photographs, film, book illustrations, paintings, artwork, 'artists' impressions' . . . even a 'dramatic re-enactment'. A regular direct approach is to have someone standing at the scene of an event, *telling* us about what we cannot *see*.

When we are discussing a particular event that has not yet taken place, we may be able to show stills or library shots of a *previous occasion* such as celebration days, processions, etc., to suggest the atmosphere, or show the principles. Sometimes a *substitute* subject can be shown, eg: of a similar type to the one being discussed.

Associated subjects are a useful ploy for 'visual padding'. When, for example, we are telling of a person's childhood in London, shots of stock tourist spots can epitomise the locale. Some subject matter can equally well suit a variety of 'padding shots', as, for example, a field of waving wheat for discussion on food crops, agriculture, insect pests, etc.

Abstract pictorial subjects can be pressed into service on almost any occasion! Atmospheric shots of rippling water, shadows, light reflections, into-sun flares, defocused images — have regular use!

126

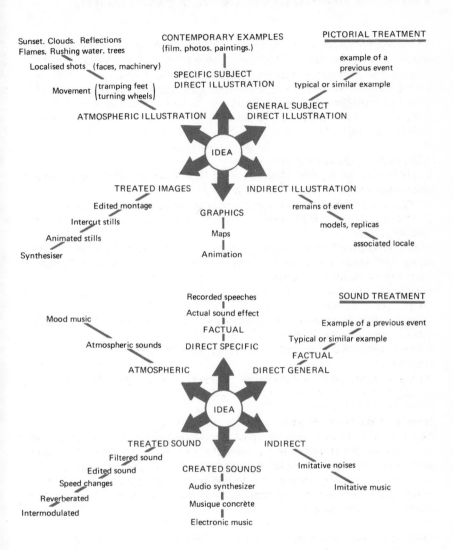

Sunset. Clouds. Reflections
Flames. Rushing water. trees

Localised shots (faces, machinery)

Movement { tramping feet
turning wheels }

ATMOSPHERIC ILLUSTRATION

CONTEMPORARY EXAMPLES
(film. photos. paintings.)

SPECIFIC SUBJECT
DIRECT ILLUSTRATION

PICTORIAL TREATMENT

example of a
previous event

typical or similar example

GENERAL SUBJECT
DIRECT ILLUSTRATION

IDEA

TREATED IMAGES

Edited montage

Intercut stills

Animated stills

Synthesiser

GRAPHICS

Maps

Animation

INDIRECT ILLUSTRATION

remains of event

models, replicas

associated locale

Mood music

Atmospheric sounds

ATMOSPHERIC

Recorded speeches

Actual sound effect

FACTUAL

DIRECT SPECIFIC

SOUND TREATMENT

Example of a previous event

Typical or similar example

FACTUAL

DIRECT GENERAL

IDEA

TREATED SOUND

Filtered sound

Edited sound

Speed changes

Reverberated

Intermodulated

CREATED SOUNDS

Audio synthesizer

Musique concrète

Electronic music

INDIRECT

Imitative noises

Imitative music

SUBJECT ILLUSTRATION

Methods of subject illustration

The most obvious way to depict a subject is to see it and to hear it directly.
Sometimes this is not possible. Sometimes a more imaginative, intriguing
approach is needed. There may be various solutions to the problem of presenting
attractive, appealing treatments in sound and picture.

Random shots lead to random audience reactions.

How to Direct Audience Attention

There are certain dictums in shot organisation. Every shot should have a purpose, however broad. It usually has a particular centre of interest. It will normally continue a foregoing theme or argument, until we want to change to a new one. If we wish to convey specific ideas, we must discourage random thought-wandering. In an advertisement for floor polish, we do not want people distracted by costume, decor, and similar side issues. How do we achieve this?

Methods of directing attention
Fundamentally, we can cause the subject to *attract the eye,* or ensure that other aspects of the shot *do not* − ie: a neutral foil.
   We can direct attention to particular features in various ways.
Exclusion: Take close shots. Avoid unwanted subjects. Simplify backgrounds.
Visual direction: Pointing with a finger, pointer, inserted arrow or circle.
Aural indication: A speaker draws attention to particular items/features.
Lighting treatment: Localised lighting; other subjects half-lit.
Composition: Using convergent line or pattern, balance, prominence through scale.
Colour: Using prominent hues against neutral or pastel hues. Using vibrant and discordant colours.
Camerawork: By differential focusing, perspective, viewpoint, camera movement.
Subject movement: Movement attracts, according to the speed, strength, direction of motion.

Value of such methods
Such a list not only reminds us of the diverse ways we can attract and hold audience attention, but it also shows how easily attention can be distracted. If, for example, a person within a background group is dressed in startling contrast to others, or fluttering a fan, a director will often exclude them, rather than let attention be drawn away from the main foreground subject.

Varying concentration
In an effectively devised production, the amount of concentration required of the audience is varied. Some shots say, 'I particularly want you to note this point', while others encourage the viewers to look around or reflect a little, or may provide a shot of a general nature that enables them to concentrate on the audio instead (ie: listening to commentary, dialogue, music). Sustained concentration causes interest to flag, and minds to wander.

Exclusion
By keeping other items out of shot, attention can be concentrated on the main subject.

Visual direction
Where rapid, unambiguous identification is essential, an indicator or marker (circle, arrow) is invaluable.

Isolation by lighting
Lighting can be arranged to isolate the required subject.

Composition
Here the eye is drawn to the main subject. The others serve as a visual support.

Creating and Controlling Interest

Audience interest is one of our primary concerns when creating a production. Without it, our show is a dead duck! Even a captive classroom audience cannot be *made* to pay attention, only encouraged!

Interesting pictures

Certain kinds of pictures have a higher associated interest than others. For instance, a shot with strongly contrasted tones is more arresting than the subtle half-tones of a high-key picture. A picture showing clear detail, encourages scrutiny, while a soft-focused version does not. Similarly, strong dynamic composition draws the eye, while weak diverse lines do not.

Progressive build-up

Intrigue your audience, but try not to puzzle or frustrate in the process (page 134). Do not put all your goods in the store window at once! Conversely, don't keep the audience waiting too long, or fail to deliver.

Information should be presented systematically, and consecutively. One idea should develop out of another. Disjointed, piecemeal facts lose their significance. If the production essentially comprises many isolated points, group them together in sections – even if their relationships are rather slight – and present them as a series of contained groups.

Avoid over-complexity, or an excess of information. Our audience needs time to examine and absorb facts. Too many facts just become an unheeded stream of words, heard but not understood.

If the shot is held for too short a time, it does not make its point. Retain it for too long, and interest inevitably fails. The optimum duration varies with the shot content, and the situation. Camera movement (or zoom) or a cut to a new viewpoint may need to be introduced to sustain interest.

Elaborate presentation

Thanks to a wide range of staging and electronic devices, considerable visual elaboration is possible – even on a small budget. Decorative effects, presentational gimmicks, and unusual displays, can certainly create interest. But all too often the viewer reacts to such ingenuity by becoming intrigued with the effect itself, rather than its purpose! One can become more preoccupied with a singer's surroundings, than with her performance. One looks at the dramatic effects, and wonders how they did them. In such circumstances, elaboration can be self-defeating.

Composition
A unified composition attracts attention to a particular subject or area.
The picture may contain an assembly of items, but the eye may not be encouraged to any particular aspect of the shot.

Visibility is not everything
Although details cannot be seen clearly, audience interest is high. We are intrigued to know more.

Influencing Audience Attitude

The presentational style adopted for the production can have a considerable influence on the audience's attitude to it.

Programme opening
Opening titles herald the intended character of the presentation. Rapid, brash, animations invite the audience lightheartedly. Archaic script and earnest, regal music, suggest historical occasions (real or fictional), to be taken seriously. The type face, its size, colour, background, etc., create a foretaste of the programme.

Staging complexity
Elaboration of decor, too, can influence how the viewer evaluates the production. Simplicity of presentation can appear clear-cut, direct, sophisticated – or sparse, frugal, uninteresting. Elaborate presentation can seem rich, interestingly complex, having great variety – or fussy, confusing, with individual features being lost.

Associations of staging
It is interesting to see how strongly the associations of a setting can influence the audience's attitude towards the subject. Where action is staged in a classroom, study, or museum, overtones of scholarship give the subject authority. But if the subject is shown in a junkyard, it becomes correspondingly devalued. A coin looks more imposing displayed on velvet, than heaped with others in a rusty tin box!

Picture key
In *high key* pictures, light tones predominate, with few dark tones. The effect (whether achieved by staging tones or lighting treatment) embues a light, fresh, brittle, gay atmosphere. *Low key* pictures, on the other hand, have a sombre, serious, dramatic connotation.

Subject importance
The subject can be made to appear important, trivial, large, small, dramatic, according to the way we shoot it. The camera height and viewpoint, speed of movement, transitions, cutting rate, can all influence the audience's attitude towards the subject.

Further factors
Being so close to the presentation ourselves, we can easily overlook the effect of various factors. Whether a presenter appears casual, reverent, indifferent or enthusiastic, can create an ambience for the entire show. The complexity of terms and speed of delivery, can affect how easily a viewer follows the argument. Even background sounds can directly modify audience attitude.

INFLUENCING AUDIENCE ATTITUDE

Titling style
The style of lettering should herald the style of the production. The type face
proclaims: dignity, occasion, fun, ruggedness, period atmosphere, etc.

Subject presentation
The presentation can affect our attitude to the subject. The subject can be
dominated, given strength, or instability.

Confusing or Frustrating Techniques

We aim to persuade and entertain our audience. But we can equally well confuse, frustrate, or antagonise them instead!

Seeing and hearing properly
Ensure that important subjects can be clearly seen – that they are not soft-focused, masked, or shadowed. Particularly where a demonstrator points to detail, it must be quite visible. Clarity is normally essential, so ensure that background tones or colours contrast well with the subject.

Try to avoid leaving the viewer feeling that he is missing something. It is better for him to be unaware, than to be tantalized as he cannot hear or see interesting subject matter.

Promises, promises
Do not have intriguing items on display in a studio scene, that the audience never sees clearly. If a guest shows a couple of items from his collection, and there are obviously many other attractive ones around, annoyance grows. If introductory remarks indicate that the viewer is going to see an item, ensure that it is not eventually eliminated due to time shortage. One easily feels cheated! Titling or graphics that are run too fast to be read, or not held long enough, are regular examples.

Annoying attitudes
Avoid introductory techniques in which the speaker does not appear to be ready for us, eg: 'I'll be with you in just a moment'. Interviewers should not be preoccupied with notes, rather than the guest.

Unseen happenings
It can be quite frustrating to be aware that action is taking place just out of shot, yet be unable to see it, for the camera is watching something else less interesting to us.

Wrong camera
Here we have a wide range of dilemmas: wrongly cued performers (page 120); a cut to unrelated subjects or viewpoints. A new person speaks, but the camera remains on an irrelevant shot. One sees just a brief shot of a subject, only to have the director cut unnecessarily to a shot of a commentator *talking about it instead!*

Puzzling shots
Try to avoid irrelevant shots, split centres of attention, and ambiguous viewpoints, where the viewer wonders what he is supposed to be looking at, or those unexplained occasions when he wonders when something is going to happen!

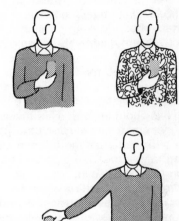

Background contrast

Hand-held items are often shot
against an unsuitable
background – a tone or hue that is
too similar to the subject, or of
confusing pattern. By holding it
against a suitable background, visual
clarity is improved.

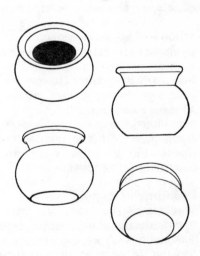

Clarity of viewpoint

Is the camera viewpoint the
optimum for the particular aspects to
be shown. Any of these *could* be
appropriate. It depends on the point
to be made.

135

Economy Thinking

Effective presentation does not necessarily involve costly, elaborate methods. 'Economy', however, does not have to produce a frugal, spartan, cheap-looking product. It is an attitude of mind; using facilities effectively, imaginatively, ingeniously and to good effect.

What is 'Economy Thinking'?
'Economy thinking' is realising that we need only to provide in the studio just what the camera is going to see (plus a little extra, perhaps, to avoid shooting off). This necessitates careful planning. The skilled designer creates an *illusion* through ingenuity.

In a dramatic presentation, a single look or gesture can prove more telling than intricate production treatment. As a camera shoots through a foreground branch, we have the impression of a forest – without needing to plant entire trees! In 'economy thinking', we start with the *effect,* and devise the most economical method of obtaining it. There are times when *silence* can engender spine-chilling tension and others when a background of street noises or bird song gives a scene absolute conviction. There is no universal rule.

Economical staging
This is staging to stimulate the imagination. It may be based on *simple mechanics* (eg: using a cyclorama and projected light patterns, or even a black background and isolated foreground furniture) or on *cost-saving constructional methods* (eg: stock scenery, revamped sets) or *special effects* (eg: chroma-key, front or rear projection).

Sometimes an associative lighting effect alone (eg: a projected window shadow, a spotlight, leaf-shadows) can convey a location or environment – especially when supported by allied background sounds.

Economy in camera treatment
Even when equipment and/or operational skill is limited, we can achieve considerable flexibility by using carefully thought-out mechanics. We may intercut sequences, shot on single cameras. Using supplementary graphics, we can engender an impression of space. Performers' movements may be used, rather than camera moves, to keep camera operations uncomplicated.

Economy of display
Graphics can be expensive. Instead of a series of individual caption or 'art' cards, therefore, (minimum size 12×9in. 31×23cm.), it may prove less costly to have the camera explore projected slides (page 89), or pan over a large sectionalised blow-up, with equal effect. Economic titling may be created easily and informally, with reusable lettering kits, or simple materials (eg: finger-drawn in wet sand).

Effective frugality
With a minimum of scenery, the shot conveys a country scene; enhanced by sound effects of bird song and wind.

Partial set
Only part of the environment is needed – so only part is built.

Light patterns
Light patterns on the cyclorama provide a cheap, adaptable, decorative background to action.

137

Don't underestimate the sound contribution.

Audio Potentials

For many TV productions, the audio is *dominant,* and the picture is a subsidiary – eg: a talks show or musical item.

Role of audio
Audio may be used to *accompany* the picture, explaining or augmenting its meaning, enriching its impact or appeal. Through music or sound effects, we can create an environmental illusion, suggesting a particular place or situation or we can build up a prevailing mood such as one of foreboding, horror, comedy.

Through audio associations, we can use carefully selected sounds to give a definite meaning to a picture that is not itself specific. For instance, the music accompanying the same display of flowers can suggest springtime, a funeral, a wedding, a ballroom. We can devise a background sound picture where in reality none exists – because the subject itself is mute eg: sculpture, insects, paintings, architecture, or where appropriate sounds were not available as with bird song or when shooting a garden scene.

Interrelating picture and sound
Over the years, various working principles have emerged to guide us when interrelating the picture and its sound. The scale and quality of the audio (perspective, acoustics) should usually match the picture. Where sound directly relates to visual action as with lip movements or effects it should be synchronized. Switching between pictures is best done to the beat of music, rather than against it, preferably at the end of a phrase. Continual cutting in time with music, becomes tedious. Sound and pictures should begin and end together, at the start and finish of a show, fading out as a musical phrase ends.

Using audio recording
Audio recordings on disc or tape are typically used in TV to provide background music, effects, and unseen speakers or commentators. They may be made for a particular production, or drawn from library sources. Used singly, or intermixed audio effects have widespread applications. They can provide, supplement, or replace sounds, both for studio action and for film/video recordings.

Audio recordings of 'voices off' (VO) 'voice over' or 'sound-over-vision' (SOV) (or on camera OC) can provide dialogue or commentary over mute film or videotape. Where a performer is not available for a live transmission, or is preoccupied at a particular moment, for instance when changing costume, his *pre-recorded* voice may substitute. A recorded voice can be used for the unseen end of a telephone 'conversation', or an unseen actor ('someone at the door'). So too, it can provide *bridging sound* when he is out of range of his microphone.

MOOD MUSIC

SYNTHETIC SOUNDS

PERIOD MUSIC

ATMOSPHERIC EFFECTS

PASTORAL
SOUNDS

MUSIC OF
THE COUNTRY

SOUND BACKGROUNDS

Audio can complement the picture
Where the subject itself is mute, or has no directly associated sound that is
appropriate, a contrived audio background can enhance the presentation. It can
be imitative, reminiscential, environmental, associative, and so on.

Unorthodox Treatment

Directors occasionally introduce unusual, unorthodox treatment to give their presentation a fresh look, to create shock, excitement, amusement, or to make it more interesting. The result can be memorable, but there is the danger, too, that it may appear contrived and too-clever.

Camera treatment
Unorthodox viewpoints include 'overhead' (through ceiling) shots, 'low shots' (ground shots, from near floor level), 'canted shots' (tilting the picture off horizontal to suggest instability).

Some 'unorthodox' techniques are really revivals of earlier photographic practices such as diffused overall or soft-edged with a clear central area. Such practices become overused periodically, as do focus-pulling (page 74), light reflections, water-reflection shots, into-the-sun shots, star filters, etc.

Lens angles can produce extreme visual effects, distorting close-ups, exaggerating or squashing space (page 26). A sudden change of lens angle to provide a 'crash zoom', or quick interswitching of lens angles to give 'zoom jumps', have their transitory value. But, like all unorthodox treatment, such techniques need careful handling, and should be introduced sparingly.

Audio treatment
Audio too, can be used unconventionally for effect. We can add echo, make the sound more reverberant, or create 'stutter effects' (multi-headed tape reproduction). We can introduce considerable audio quality changes with filtering or modulation effects, or alter pitch and speed from 'chipmunk' speech to slowed-down effects. Audio voices for creatures from outer space, give full rein to the imagination.

Lighting treatment
Decorative light-patterns should be used systematically, especially if they are intended to have associative connotations such as to remind one of leafy shadows, or rippling water. Do not just provide a random scattering of unrelated blobs and streaks, and hope that it will gel into something meaningful, but aim at a cohesive, unified effect overall.

Coloured light always poses problems of artistic taste. Colour harmony, or colour relationships that are acceptable in one situation, may be quite out of place in another. Coloured light on people grouped around a pop singer may be vibrant and in key with the mood of the occasion. But the style would be totally unacceptable for a serious song.

Light movement, too, can add an exciting piquancy, or become an annoying distraction. Light flashing to a musical beat, flashing signs, travelling spotlights, flicker effects, enliven the right occasion – but can destroy it when inappropriately used.

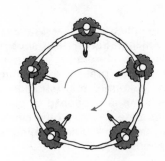

Overhead shot

An overhead view can reveal decorative effect, grouping and movement.

Alternatively, the overhead shot can give the audience a dramatic overall view, so that they can see the intruder behind the door, and the unsuspecting newcomer.

Ground shot

An extremely dramatic viewpoint that can be achieved by shooting into a low mirror and using a very low camera mounting, or staging the scene on an elevated area.

Canted shot

The canted (tilted) shot remains one of the most effective ways of conveying instability, fear, madness, etc.

Continuity

Most people are familiar with the fundamental problem of 'continuity' in film making. Scenes are shot as convenient, over a period of time, usually out of running order, so one has to ensure that when cut together they present a continuous, coherent presentation. Cigarettes, drinks, costume, etc., should not appear to change between shots. Where time is supposed to elapse, there should be appropriate signs such as time changes on a clock, aging people or the passing seasons. In any discontinuous filming or videotaping for TV, similar considerations arise.

Regular continuity problems

Pictorial continuity is the need to ensure that intercut shots fit together visually, avoiding dissimilar tonal balance eg: intercut high and low-key.

Spatial continuity prevents the viewer from losing his sense of direction or location on cuts. This happens during 'reverse angle cutting'.

Attention continuity ensures that as we switch to a new shot, the viewer does not have to search around for the new centre of interest.

Relationship continuity avoids mismatched cuts that might jump-cut the subject around the frame.

Temporal continuity makes sure that the audience maintains a good sense of the passage of time, and the time-relationship of events such as the feeling that dramatic action is taking place within a single day, or flashback techniques.

Event continuity is necessary when people make exits or entrances out of shot. It is disconcerting to have someone standing in a particular place, and find on switching back to him after an intermediate graphic, that he is now unexpectedly relocated in a new area.

Deliberate discontinuity

The TV audience is too sophisticated nowadays, due largely to motion picture viewing, to need to see each step of routine actions. If an automobile stops outside a house, it is sufficient to show just that, and cut to the caller ringing the house door bell. All the intermediary action as he leaves the car, walks up the path, etc. can be omitted. By cutting out unnecessary action, the pace is tautened, time saved, and the boringly obvious avoided. This use of *filmic space* and *filmic time* is applied universally.

Similarly, in a cookery demonstration, we do not wait for each stage of a recipe to be prepared and/or cooked, but show examples of each step leading up to the completed item. The audience accepts the fact that it is not seeing every moment of the process. So, too, when *cutaway shots* are used (page 158), we can make considerable jumps in time (and place) without puzzling the audience – or even making them aware of the interruption.

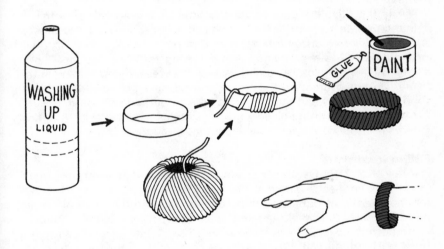

CONTINUITY

Broken continuity
When retaking action, avoid broken continuity due to articles having been consumed or repositioned throughout the original take. Action and positions should be matched.

Deliberate discontinuity
The various stages of making a decorative bangle from a plastic bottle section wrapped with string. Showing isolated steps, saves the time and tedium of watching the entire process in continuity.

Using Titling

Titling has many important applications in TV production – programme titles, identification of persons, places or time, displaying terms such as parts of a plant, and lettering, credits or cast lists.

Titling design
Titling methods themselves are very varied. Some are extremely adaptable, while others provide an over-familiar, stereotyped result. Some are instantly alterable such as electronic character generators or, clip-on letters, while others, such as slides, cannot be modified.

Unlike slides in a caption machine, titling set up in front of a studio camera has the advantage that we can adjust its size and position in the frame to suit another shot. But it ties up another camera.

While the titles designer (graphics) aims to avoid a type face that is of inappropriate style, or does not televise well because it is too thin, or ornamental, or of unsuitable tone or contrast, the director also must look out for certain problems. Avoid having lettering too small (not below 1/10–1/25 picture height). Avoid an excess of information in the frame. Do not overcrowd the frame and cause edge cut-off. Maintain good contrast between titling and its background when superimposing. Try to avoid intercutting closely matching titles as when adding details progressively, because accurate alignment throughout is unlikely.

Titling treatment
We can often improve clarity or impact of lettering by electronic treatment. Commonest, perhaps, is *black edging,* a form of edge-enhancement that puts a black border around lettering. Variations are available, including white-edging and 'dropped' or 'drop' shadows. Using such a device, it is even possible to see white lettering against a white background, but letters must be open and simple for good readability. Electronic matting (overlay) enables lettering to be 'punched solid' into an existing picture, avoiding the interaction of tones and colours that occurs in superimposed titling. Further electronic circuitry enables one to take white on black titling, and insert chosen colours eg: producing red letters/yellow background. More complex systems can even provide different hues for various shades of grey.

Readability
Keep titling to a minimum. If there is too much to read, people will not bother to do so! It must be appropriately timed to prevent distraction. Read all titling aloud (twice) to ensure that the slowest viewer can assimilate it. Very fast title sequences (single or crawl roller captions) easily become ridiculous. If an announcer has to read matter clearly displayed on the screen ensure that the reading is *accurate.*

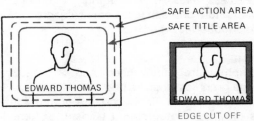
SAFE ACTION AREA
SAFE TITLE AREA
EDWARD THOMAS

EDGE CUT OFF

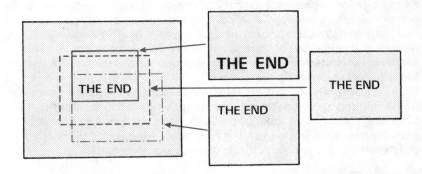
THE END

THE END

THE END

THE END

HEAD TITLE

SUB-TITLE

LEFT TITLE

CENTRAL TITLE

TITLING

Titling safe area
To avoid parts of titling being lost beyond the edge of the average TV screen, make sure that it falls within the safe title-area. (Action should be kept within the safe action-area limits.)

Titling card size
If a title is set within a fairly large black background, the camera can frame it in various ways.

Title positions
Titling can be localised to prevent its obscuring the subject, or for visual variety.

145

Graphics are pictorial captions.

Using Graphics

Graphics have endless uses in illustrating TV productions – maps, diagrams, cartoons, photo shots of locations, subjects too large to bring to the studio or to shoot effectively, etc.

Types of graphics
Card-mounted graphics are widely used, and offer relative economy and flexibility. Large graphics (such as photo blow-ups) are expensive to produce, usually mounted on flats, and integrated into the scenic design. Graphics may be photographed (slides), or filmed (animation stand) where a complex selective or animated sequence is involved. Slide graphics or photographs may be projected, and shot by the studio camera *either as a whole or in part.* Where telops or caption-scanners are used to televise opaques or slides, the *whole* image will fill the frame, and only by electronic masking *(wipe-patterns, inlay)* can sections be obliterated by uncover or cover-up treatment. We cannot make part of the slide fill the screen.

Animated graphics can be achieved by various methods: frame-by-frame filming or videotaping, using moving sections, inter-camera switching or lighting changes. Cost normally precludes elaborate animation, but it can be useful to give visual interest (to graphs, maps, charts) and, to show how subjects work or are constructed.

Advice on using graphics
Keep important details in the 'safe area' away from picture edges. Avoid small detail and fussy shading particularly fine, close lines, over-elaboration and crowded information. The ideal graphic has a matte flat surface with no cockling, buckling, curling, blisters. Photographs should generally have good detail and tonal gradation, from highlights to shadows. Avoid high contrast, soot-and-whitewash prints.

Avoid rapid intercutting between a series of captions on studio floor stands. Even one false or slow change can wreck a sequence, and shaking or misaligned shots are all too likely.

It is easier for a cameraman to zoom than to dolly (track) to and from a caption if he is to maintain sharp focus. If you intend zooming into detail, remember that the cameraman must usually check and focus his shot in the zoomed-in position. Otherwise focus errors can arise. Cameramen should *always* shoot head on to a graphic, or distortions are inevitable. Light reflections or glare on glossy graphics may sometimes be remedied by *slight* re-angling.

Ideally, a graphic should be in the proportions 4×3. If it is not, one has to select a portion, so losing the rest, or mount it on a black card and shoot the total graphic with its black surround, obtaining a smaller image. Where, a camera has to shoot graphics of *different shapes and sizes,* you must allow time for recomposition between each.

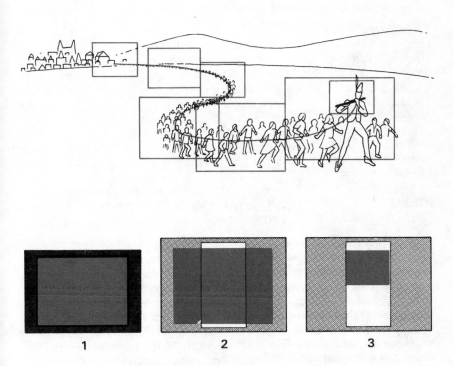

1   2   3

GRAPHICS

Typical graphics sizes (4 units across, by 3 units down)

cms.	in.	
30·5 × 23	12 × 9	Smallest for convenient handling
40 × 30	16 × 12	
61 × 46	24 × 18	Larger sizes are unwieldy

Thickness of support card (minimum) 2mm. ($\frac{1}{16}$")

Exploring graphics

By exploring a detailed graphic with the camera, a story can be told while providing continual visual change.

Aspect ratio

1. Only a graphic in 4 by 3 proportions will fit the TV frame.   2. A tall narrow graphic can be shot as a whole but with black side borders.   3. It can be shot in selected areas.

147

Using Film

For the director there are still numerous differences between film and video camera production systems.

Directing differences

Film offers the director a compact, highly mobile, relatively trouble-free medium. Although there are no visual checks, multi-takes usually ensure success. All editing decisions and selections are made after shooting is over. He has the close guidance and advice of his single cameraman and, later, his film editor. We generally find that filmed presentations have a faster pace, with more frequent changes in viewpoint (set-up) and location than electronic shooting. Filming can be studio or location based, but the shooting-rate (amount of usable material shot daily) is considerably lower than when video cameras are used.

Shooting with *video cameras,* more decisions have to be made more quickly. The director himself guides multi-camera operations. Shooting is less fragmented. Post-production editing is more basic.

Film in production

Typical occasions when film is used to *augment* continuous studio production include location shooting to extend studio action, impracticable or dangerous items (fire), once-only action (wreckage), make-up transformations, major wardrobe changes (wet to dry), time-state changes (old reverting to new), library shots and time-lapse.

Film libraries maintain extensive collections of *library* or *stock shots* that can be integrated into a production. These include events, personalities, special effects, locations and processes. Apart from occasions when it would be quite impracticable to shoot or re-stage new material, stock shots provide convenient, economical picture sources. Where material is mute, suitable sound effects are added.

The main unavoidable drawback of such shots, however, is that certain often-used subjects can become too familiar, and deterioration in quality (colour, tonal range, definition, blemishes) can prevent their matching unobtrusively with other material.

Because *film* is physically vulnerable to damage, one uses an earlier proof print for studio rehearsals, and the final, higher-grade *show print* for taping (transmission). Negative film has been televised (electronically reversed) but it is normally too precious to risk.

Film inserts into a studio show are usually preceded by 'standard' leaders, containing numbered frames showing one second intervals, to aid cueing. However, when cutting frequently to and from a series of film clips, it may be preferable to insert black leader *(blanking)* of suitable durations between them, and leave the film projector running. Film rewind time may have to be allowed for during rehearsal, particularly if a separate sound track is used.

148

Comparing TV and film shooting

	TV	FILM
Flexibility/Mobility/Ruggedness.	Fairly low for *high quality* pictures. Power needed, often weighty, bulky, associated equipment. Usually cabled.	Very high. Lightweight. Compact. No power problems. No cables.
Quantity of skilled man power and equipment, back-up support.	Often quite high.	Can be very low.
Cost. Material consumed.	Equipment high cost. Virtually nil. Videotape re-usable, except preserved masters.	Fairly high equipment Film continually expended.
Visual checks on shooting.	Immediate full check of final product. Seen by production group. Focusing, composition, continuously visible.	None during shooting; only after processing (time delays, costs, uncertainties). Rough prints (rushes, dailies) have to be checked and rectified. Focusing by measurement (and optical).
Image quality colour control.	Immediately adjustable. Continuously monitored.	Director can only assess eventual prints.
Production techniques.	Can be continuous or segmented; live (immediate) or recorded (delayed) presentation.	Essentially segmented, intermittent shooting. Post-production editing.
Number of cameras.	1 to 5 cameras used in combined set-up.	Usually 1; using a series of separate set-ups, and with repeat takes.
Duration of takes.	Action may be continuous. Take may last several minutes, using intercut cameras.	Usually single camera shooting with brief duration takes. Maximum take eg: 10 min.
Director's control over shooting.	Continuous. Can see and guide cameras.	Relies largely on interpretation of cameraman.
Check on production.	Can watch continuously; can re-run VTR to check.	Estimated only. No direct checks. Precautionary retakes.
Work required on shot material.	Show can be complete, ready for transmission after shooting; or can be edited.	All shot film needs sorting, classifying, arranging in order, before editing.
Editing.	Immediate. Simple. Post-production videotape editing fairly time consuming and costly. Subtle editing possible, but laborious on simpler VTR systems.	Editing essential to produce a consecutive reproduction. Very subtle editing quite practicable. Only 'cuts' made simply. Other transitions made by labs.
Picture quality.	At best, high. Continually adjustable for optimum. Performance can change.	Can be high. Marred by blemishes. Quality only adjustable during processing.

Using Videotape

Videotape is magnetically recorded, and can be selectively or bulk-erased for re-use.

Methods of use

We can use videotape in several ways: *continuous recording* straight through, like a live transmission; in *parts,* scene-by-scene; in *segments,* brief takes, shot-by-shot. While continuous recording produces a complete package, ready for transmission, it may well lack polish, or have uneven appeal. A production that has been recorded in short segments, however, may need considerable re-recording *(dubbing)* or addition of music and effects *(laying tracks)* to provide the final composite videotape. Picture quality deteriorates in any dubbing process, and when the *master tape* (first generation) has been dubbed (second gen.) and a copy made of that copy (third gen.), the results can be degraded.

Videotape offers many productional opportunities: *Recording in any order* (to suit convenience, make-up or wardrobe changes); *correction* of faults in action, lines, technical errors, by re-recording and editing; *improvements* in presentation (a better 'take', tighter pace, omit pauses, censorship); *compensation* for shortages of equipment, space or time, overcoming staging or talent availability problems; *effects* that are impracticable in the studio (eg: fire), unreliable (knife throw), once-only events (explosion, wreckage); *video treatment* such as transfer to video disc, or colour synthesizer effects; *backing copy* (protection copy) recording a programme in duplicate, in case one copy has technical faults (a customary procedure); *dubbing film* where a valuable print may break on the air, or to add subtitling, translation, commentary, music.

Videotape editing

Basically, videotape editing involves either recording new programme material over the original section on the tape *(insert edit)*, or dubbing-off by replaying selected passages to a second, videotape recorder. In *assemble (assembly) editing* we record a series of separate sections one after another, so that they are conjoined on replay.

Automatic and semi-automatic systems exist, to make VT editing quicker and easier. In one system a pushbutton cue-marker enables us to put an audio 'beep' on to the tape's guide track. Replay allows a position check of the cue-point. Then, replaying again for the editing, the machine switches itself at the cue-point, to record new material.

Video disc recording

Well in evidence in network sports telecasts, the video disc can store a mute 36 sec. (72 sec. max.) programme segment. It provides various facilities, including sequential repeats, fast or slow replay (speed adjustable), reverse motion, freeze frame, frame-by-frame advance.

150

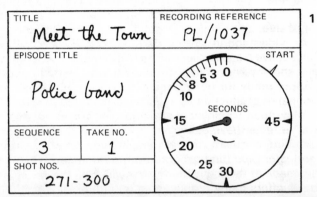

VIDEORECORDING

1. VT slate

The VT slate or clock is recorded at the start of the main recording, and major sequences. Often preceded by test signals (tone and colour-bars), it provides programme identification, and recording details. The clock is started at −30 sec. (or −1 min.), to give time for the videorecorder to reach full speed, and to provide a timed countdown for programme cueing.

An electronic leader from a special generator, can be used similarly, for timing in-cues.

2. Time-code identification

For sophisticated VT editing, a *digital time-code* is recorded alongside the video, its numbers identifying the hour/minute/second/frame, at the instant of recording. These code numbers can be displayed, and used to identify required editing points. In one method the director takes away a helical-scan dubbing-copy of his show, incorporating the picture with superimposed code numbers. He scrutinises this, making editing decisions. Later, at the actual editing session with the master tape, his chosen coded cue-points enable the original passages to be located — manually or automatically.

151

Using Electronic Insertion

Using electronic wizardry, we can punch a 'hole' in a *master shot,* and insert there the exactly corresponding area of another picture (the *background shot).* The simplest system *(special effects generator, inlay)* can usually only insert within a selection of geometrical shapes *(wipes, inserts).* A more sophisticated system *(chroma-key, CSO, colour separation overlay)* inserts any shape automatically, even shadows, wherever a special *keying hue* (usually blue or yellow) appears in the master shot. The *background* shot can contain any hues, and come from any video source.

Chroma-key offers many opportunities for staging economies, and for unique visual effects. However, it must be applied and adjusted systematically if we are to avoid perspective and scale errors, edge-tearing, and spurious breakthrough. Both *hard-edged* (sharp) and *soft-edged* (diffused) switching circuitry is available; the latter being less critical to adjust.

Applications

Display areas can be produced by either electronic system. As a general guide, we can say that normally people can only move 'in front of' a chroma-keyed insertion, and 'behind' an effects generator (inlay) insert. When chroma-keyed, the display area can cover the whole background, or can be confined to a local area of any shape.

Scenic backgrounds can be provided by chroma-key, replacing built staging in the studio. So we can place a person in the studio 'within' a photograph or painting. If the performer is to appear full-length within the background, the *keying hue* must extend over the floor area, as well as behind the subject. *Localised scenic insertion* can supply backgrounds 'behind' car and room windows. Remember, though, film and videotape used for moving backgrounds are of limited duration; and for driving scenes, subject action may need to relate to them.

Bizzare effects such as giants, dwarfs, and strange perspective are so easily achieved, that the problem lies in preventing them, and maintaining *correct* scale and perspective! People can be made to 'walk around' inside models (miniatures). Should the occasion require it, people and objects (all or part of them) can be made to appear or vanish. It is possible to switch the background scene, while retaining the foreground subject, or vice versa. One can create 'instant' live paintings simply by brushing a foreground surface with the keying hue.

Where a production has a regular introductory opening sequence on film or VT, this can include chroma-key patches, into which a picture of current studio subjects such as that day's guest can be inserted.

In the most elaborate chroma-key applications, multiple images can be created by systematic intermixes – either simultaneously, or by re-recording.

152

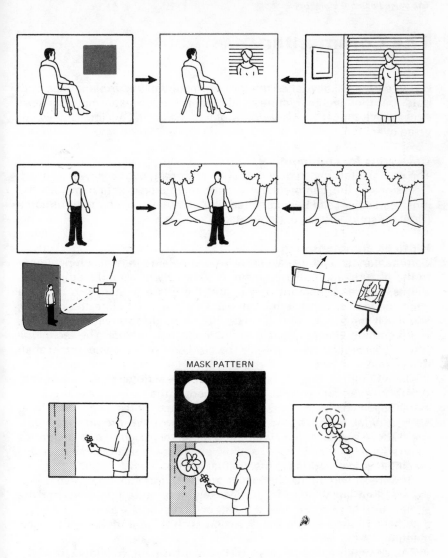

MASK PATTERN

ELECTRONIC INSERTION

Local insertion with chroma-key (CSO)
A patch of the *keying hue* in Cam. 1 scene, enables us to insert a corresponding area of another shot on Cam. 2 (the rest of that shot is lost).

Overall insertion with chroma-key
A total background of the keying hue behind the subject, inserts it *'into'* the picture.

Special effects generator (inlay) insertion
Using a mask pattern, we can insert a selected section of camera shots into others to show detail and an overall view in one picture.

153

The Commentary

Commentary usually takes the form of observations, explanations, and data on the events pictured. Although the speaker may be seen occasionally, most of his work is *out of vision* (OOV) (off camera, or voice over, VO).

Occasions for commentary
The commentator is an observer or an informant on the viewer's behalf. Occasionally the commentary accompanies studio action but for the most part, it is used behind edited film or videotape, and with remotes (OBs) for sport, display or pageants.

Hints on commentating
Commentary should usually serve as a supplementary accompaniment to the picture, and not overwhelm it. This may prove difficult in sports events, where excitement grows, and there is a tendency to describe what the viewer can see for himself. One must not state the obvious, and insult the viewer's intelligence. Yet, without observations, the less well informed viewer might overlook important factors. The technique is to *explain* which player it is, or the problems of the game, rather than to *describe*.

Commentaries are of two basic types – scripted and unscripted. Where programme material is spontaneous, the usual procedure, after initial research, is to work from abbreviated notes – eg: identifying players, brief histories, local colour – and to have pre-arranged *out-cues*. These words, agreed with the director, are used to cue illustrative inserts (graphics, film, VTR), and so avoid the embarrassment of unpredicted verbal lead-ins to inserts that are not ready.

Beware of comments that occur too early, introducing an event that we are then left waiting for. Conversely, it is quite frustrating for the audience to hear comments that lag behind events – particularly when they have missed seeing the occasion such as at a multi-event sports meeting.

The commentator's voice should be heard clearly and not in 'reading' style. Spurious noises easily develop from script rustling. Unstaple the script, and drop numbered sheets to the floor, or slide them aside. Noisy surroundings can be suppressed by a special noise-cancelling mike. Otherwise, a fairly close mike position is best adopted, taking care to avoid 'puffing' onto the mike. Use a wind shield, and always make a voice *level-check* with the audio engineer beforehand.

Commentators use various forms of cueing systems (page 120) including manual, visual, and audible cues. Cueing from a monitor screen can be equally effective, providing there is no likelihood of confusion or ambiguity such as similar shots that mislead the cueing point.

Out-of-vision commentary
Where the commentator is never seen, he may be located in an announce-booth, or in a corner of the studio.

Desk monitor
Where the commentator is seen in shot at a desk, a small monitor may be hidden within it, unseen by the camera.

In-shot monitor
A nearby monitor shows film or videotape on which the studio talent comments. Where a colour monitor is used in shot, it requires careful colour re-balance for it to look correct on camera.

Single Performer

The single performer show covers a number of regular situations – introducer, presenter, lecturer, commentator, demonstrator (page 166) or singer. No other production format provides such close communication with the audience as the single performer – or a bigger bore if the presentation is inept.

Looking at the camera
Always make it clear whether the performer is to address the audience continuously, or only during certain sequences. A lone singer, for example, may be 'overseen' by the camera, or look directly towards it, according to how the performance is presented. If a person is to play to camera, he must know which camera is on him, and how close the shot is. Where a prompter aid (or a picture monitor) is used, it must not cause him to maintain an off-camera stare, and he must be able to read it easily.

Movement
Keep action simple, particularly for talent who are not familiar with TV studio mechanics. Make the *moment* for actions clear (a series of separate cues for a sequence of moves if necessary), and ensure that the performer has no doubt about the various positions he is to move to (page 118).

Over-mobility looks fidgety. Many directors move the single performer around excessively, standing, sitting, walking, leaning, gesticulating, turning to a new camera viewpoint just to create a visual change. The secret is to make any move appear rational, and naturally motivated – preferably not by discomfort! Don't let a person wander around. Give him definite location points instead.

Shots
Head-on static shots are dull. Try to introduce dolly (tracking) or zoom shots to vary interest, emphasise points, adjust concentration. However, do not change viewpoints to excess. A camera may justifiably move round to take over-shoulder shots, but laborious repositioning to get these will spoil the impact of the treatment (page 80).

Let the talent know when his actions affect your shots. Do not assume that, because he held a jar so that we could read the label during rehearsal, he will do just that on recording. Show him the problems, and if necessary, how he can check his presentation on a nearby monitor.

Sometimes we may want a performer to wait a beat (a silent count of 'one') between saying something, and showing an item to the camera, or before making a move. This can help to give time for a camera to settle on a shot, or to change to another viewpoint.

SINGLE PERFORMER

Angling the desk
Straight-on frontal or side views can look posed and awkward. Instead, angle
the desk slightly.

Subject movement
The performer should not be kept in a static position for too long. But in moving
and repositioning him, always consider whether the result is appropriate.

157

'Just people talking'. But it needs careful thought.

Interviews

Try to prepare guests before they meet the camera. Make them welcome, agree on the main points to be discussed, and time available.

In the studio
Save the guest the tedium of sitting under hot lights while you set up shots, by using stand-ins before his arrival. Mark chair positions. A brief trial run with a specimen topic can help to settle the talent, provide sound-level checks and may reveal idiosyncracies (leaning back or forward, arm movements) for which to allow when shooting. But avoid rehearsing the interview itself. It reduces spontaneity. Ensure that the guest has seen in advance any film or tape inserts being referred to, but prevent his being preoccupied with nearby picture monitors.

The interviewer has a considerable influence on the effectiveness of the production. He should draw on researchers' notes *(fact sheet,* or *background card),* and not seem to be preoccupied with studio mechanics, or the next item. Always appearing interested in replies, he should ask related questions rather than the next one on the list. Information should seem to come from the guest. In general, the interviewer avoids feeding back to the guest data on where he was born, educated, worked, etc., unless it is in doubt and needs checking. Such details are better included in an introduction.

Most interviews gain polish from being recorded, for conversation lapses and important aspects may be overlooked. Some directors like to record a timed interview, and retake faulty passages. Others prefer recording lengthy, discussive interviews, from which the most interesting sections are then extracted by editing.

Location interview
An inexperienced guest feels less tension when interviewed at home, or his place of work, than in formal studio surroundings. A single camera (film or video) is often used, concentrating on the guest, dollying or zooming to vary the length of shot. (Avoid shooting a long static interview on a hand-held camera wherever possible.)

After the interview, two-shots are taken of repeat questions, to be edited in where necessary, together with 'reaction' *nod shots* (smiles and head nodding), and *cutaways* of questions. Avoid having moving lips in these shots. These inserted shots, or *cut-ins,* help us to avoid the monotony of the viewer watching a continuous unchanging shot, enable us to make cuts in boring or irrelevant sections, and to bridge any breaks in conversation (page 48). Moreover, the interview can now be trimmed to an exact length.

Where someone cannot get to the studio, an interviewer may speak to an inset screen or picture monitor showing his guest.

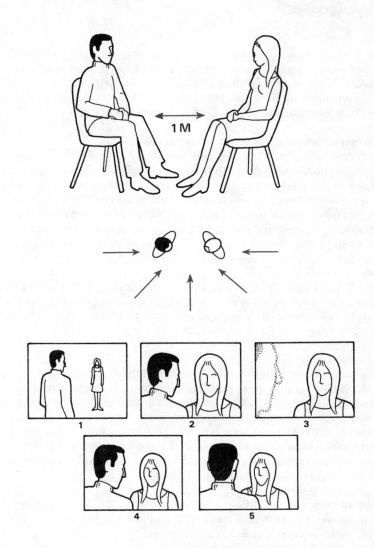

INTERVIEW

Talent positions
If people sit within about a metre (yard) of each other, an optimum variety of shots becomes possible. More widely spaced (page 83) and frontal two-shots are impracticable.

Over-shoulder shots
The proportions of over-shoulder shots are important. 1. Too distant. 2. Too similar in size. 3. Too close. These are rarely satisfactory. 4. A slightly angled front person (nose just visible) is preferable to a back-of-head view, 5.

Talk Shows

Talk shows take several forms: a 'dissenting group' with two or more conflicting speakers and a chairman; a 'press conference', where a panel questions an important guest; a 'team' group, (an assembly discussing an issue); an 'audience discussion' with a speaker or a panel of experts; or a 'running analysis' of a special event (such as an election).

Presenter/Chairman/Link-Man/Anchorman
Like an interview, the central guide (variously titled) of a discussion show needs research briefing, to be familiar with production aims and details, to guide topic discussion, be aware of time allowances, and to introduce both the subjects and guests to the viewer. He controls discipline, prevents undue dominance, steers discussion back to the subject, maintaining it along prescribed lines. He will rescue, improvise, stall, anticipate problems, and generally use controlled initiative.

Layout
Groups of chairs look unattractive, and casual seating makes good shot continuity and grouping difficult. So 'talks tables' and desk set-ups were evolved in talk shows to keep people close together yet provide the variations of single, two and group shots.

Typical shooting
Most discussion treatment comprises these basic shots, with some *cross shots (side shots)* and possible *over-shoulder shots,* with the risk of masking if the foreground person moves around; sustained individual shots soon pall, so *reaction shots* are intercut. These establish rapport or antipathy between speakers. But avoid the vacant gaze, preoccupied or disinterested look – unless that is an appropriate comment! Shots of hands nervously tapping or intertwined fingers, are a visual garnish that seldom contributes much to the presentation.

Ad lib discussion
Few talk shows are shot-scripted. Instead, a shooting-plan is prepared, with cameras located strategically over a wide angle to provide selective shots as needed. The plan might go: Cam. 1, a wide-angle cover shot, and chosen pairs of speakers; Cam. 2, the presenter, and CUs of certain people; Cam. 3, the other close-ups, entrances, exits, opening and closing titles. This avoids two cameras offering similar shots, or none of an interjecting speaker. Variations are introduced as necessary, avoiding zooming in vision.

When an audience is involved in questions or comments, the principals can be arranged in the front row, or people can talk in an agreed order, or the chairman may indicate individuals before they speak. This avoids cameras and mike having to search for the speaker.

TALK SHOWS

Layouts

Layouts for talk shows can be arranged to provide *individual impact* (people in chairs), or to create *segmented unity* (people are broken up into sections), or to present *group unity* (in an assembly). The interviewer (I) or chairman/link-man/anchorman, has a coordinating role. Each layout has its particular convenience and adaptability. Desks add a formality or sense of occasion.

Newscasts

Newscasts have evolved over the years, to take on relatively standardised formats. In practice, their mechanics are akin to those found in various 'omnibus' presentations such as sports round-ups in which a central anchorman introduces a series of inserted items, sometimes providing a commentary, and always prepared to improvise.

Presentation fundamentals

Reading roller prompters, newscasters appear to be speaking directly to the viewer. Desk cards or a script *(copy)* serve as emergency notes in the event of prompter failure, but reading scripts to camera can produce a preoccupied, or impromptu air. An earpiece or a desk phone provide communication with the director. Monitors show the on-air transmitted picture, and a preview of the next item's leader.

Most newscasts involve narration to camera, a series of brief film stories, videotape sequences, slides, graphics and titling *(super cards)*. Sometimes there are hand-overs (switches) to live inserts from remotes (OBs) with on-the-spot commentators.

The essence of good presentation is organisation. An up-to-date running order is essential (including latest items and deletions), complete with actual durations, *in-cues* and *out-cues* for each section. The timing of entries and 'outs' can be affected by the speed and accuracy of the newscaster's reading. Timing cues in the script (prompter) margin assist the newsreader in keeping the dialogue in step with the picture, and to introduce pauses of appropriate lengths. *Ad libs* are not welcome, if there is a need to achieve precise cueing-in of insert material, for cueing is taken from marked places in the script.

In the event of a film break, or the non-appearance of a film or VTR item, a reserve story is held on a standby machine, the newscaster having anticipatory reserve announcements for these stories.

Presentation techniques

For the director, emphasis is on accurate cueing of the right source, and coordinating contributors. The camera positions are static, and shots are modified by zooming. Subtitles (identifying people, places or time) are added strategically, when they will not detract from an important point in the story.

Most stations make extensive use of chroma key (CSO) to provide a background to the newscaster, or a 'wall display' beside him. Others utilise *in-shot* monitors, and/or cut away to insert sources, rather than integrate them into the studio picture.

It is as well, where using chroma key, to avoid the instant 'appearances' and 'transformations' that arise when switching foreground subjects (newscasters) and retaining the same background shot. The effect is bizarre and adds nothing to the presentation.

NEWSCASTS

As the Newscaster sees it
Although he appears at ease talking directly to the audience, the Newscaster is
in reality working to a carefully timed presentation surrounded by various aids:
prompter, picture monitors, clock, floor-manager, standby script, cue-light,
desk phone to director.

Illustrated Talk

Illustrated talks represent an economical, flexible, and highly adaptable method of presenting a variety of subjects.

Methods
Where budgets permit, we may take a camera to a location, and shoot the production (or inserts) there. But location shooting has its limitations (page 180), and all the required material may not be available at one place. Apart from space restrictions and noise problems, we may have difficulties in avoiding unwanted adjacent items, and in isolating our particular subjects.

Consequently, illustrated talks usually bring the material to the studio in the form of photographs, slides, film, videotape, specimens, artwork and models. By intercutting between source material, and exploring stills (zooming, panning over, insetting details, animation), the director can build up an effective presentation, with an interlinking commentator.

Presentation formats
Regular formats include: the *neutral* or non-associative setting, with desk, graphics, wall-charts, models, etc., the *atmospheric* setting, suggesting a study, library, office, hobbies room; and the *locational* set, simulating laboratory, factory museum, etc. The speaker may be an expert who is, hopefully, at ease with TV mechanics, or an experienced TV presenter working from a script devised by others.

Staging should be visually interesting, yet without eye-catching clutter. Careful viewpoints can prevent viewers from seeing and becoming preoccupied with items used later in the programme. Contrived shots are out of place, though, for emphasis is on the clear presentation of information, rather than pictorial effect.

Where a speaker is referring to book illustrations, we can shoot these as he examines them, or as separate graphics or slides, or as post-production close-ups edited in later. Over-shoulder shots of hand-held items are often obscured by head or hands or shadows. We can seldom get close enough to see detail. The item is often held unsteadily, and may catch the light and so bleach out details. All book illustrations should have markers to avoid fumbling or wrong selection. Try not to flick over pages that the viewer is not going to be shown properly.

It is often better to present simplified graphics than detailed, multi-labelled illustrations – particularly for maps, sectional drawings, pages of statistics, half-tone photographs of apparatus, and similar subjects that do not translate well to the TV screen. Remember too, that very close shots of existing illustrations may not necessarily show sufficient detail, but show such defects as strobing, patterning, dot structure and detailless shadows.

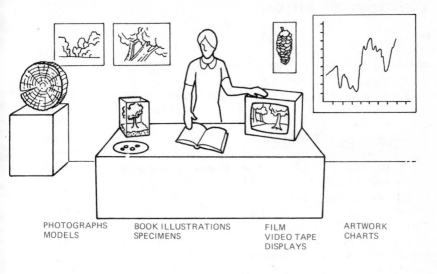

PHOTOGRAPHS   BOOK ILLUSTRATIONS   FILM   ARTWORK
MODELS   SPECIMENS   VIDEO TAPE   CHARTS
                                             DISPLAYS

ILLUSTRATED TALK

Studio talk
The production is a composite of recorded material interlinked with studio
presentation. The camera explores specimens, models, illustrations, graphics,
etc.

The illustrated talk on location
A talk 'on location' (real or reconstructed), illustrates fashions, using paintings,
book illustrations, a girl in period dress, etc.

165

Demonstrations

Demonstrations can be used to show *variety* (such as different designs of Spanish armour), to show *development* (synthesis – how a seed becomes a tree), to show *construction (analysis – breaking down items into constituent parts), or to show actions and reactions* (as in chemical experiments).

Organising demonstrations
Always get full practical information about demonstration subjects or materials before they reach the studio – dimensions, power supplies, precautions, process durations, insurance, transport, etc.

Do not try to cover too wide a subject in a single show, or tell too much. Is it to be a general survey, or describe a particular feature? Sectionalise its various aspects in a rational development. Demonstrations should show details clearly, show relationships between parts, reveal differences in appearance, provide comparisons, compare style or methods, show change and so on. So our production techniques are chosen to achieve these particular aims.

Arrange the demonstration as a *consecutive* coverage or display. Try to avoid moving to and fro over items, or having surplus items in shot such as those which are already used, or being used later.

Unless the demonstrator actually needs to handle graphics (maps, charts) these are usually better arranged on caption/graphics stands shot by other cameras. Hand-held captions can provide focus and shine problems, and are best slid aside, rather than turned over.

Preoccupied with mechanics, a demonstrator may not be able to follow a prompter. So dialogue and durations are liable to vary. To avoid having to prune an over-long show, or extend a short one, *buffer items (cushions)* may be included that can be expanded or contracted as time allows. When showing development or construction, it is usually more time-saving and predictable, to have a series of separate stages already prepared, rather than attempt to carry through a real-time demonstration (page 143). Thus, we can show the steps in preparing a meal, with examples of each stage, rather than videotape the entire operation and edit it, to fit the allocated period.

Always check apparatus on arrival, and before and after use, and ensure that it is carefully collected, and returned or stored after use.

Demonstration in close-up
We have met the various problems of close-up viewpoints, so let us summarise them here: Hold subjects still, use locating marks, avoid masking detail using a pointer rather than a finger, avoid distortion, keep movements slow and restricted. Put items into position in medium shots, then cut to a close-up view. Avoid the fast zoom-in, or putting items in or out of frame. When in doubt, cut to a wider shot.

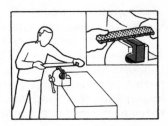

The inset
An inset enables us to show detail
and overall effect simultaneously.

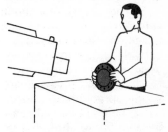

Working to the camera
Whenever possible, the
demonstrator should work to the
camera.

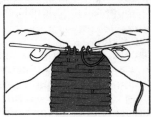

Camera viewpoint
Sometimes the demonstrator cannot
work to the camera. Aim to get the
best viewpoint available in the
circumstances.

Comparisons
To compare situations, a split screen
can show before and after
conditions.

Music and Dance

Music and dance have certain common presentational characteristics, for each involves both *group effort,* and *individual performance.*

Techniques

In music and dance, we can present the subject for *effect,* eg: compositional patterns, decorative shadows and dynamic movements, or to impart *information,* eg: instrumental fingering, playing techniques, foot movements. Perhaps, a mixture of each. Camera treatment should be in keeping with the tempo and mood of work.

Picture transitions should be appropriately timed, and at a speed to suit music and action – quick cutting for fast, exciting sequences, slow mixes for more languid, sedate passages. Split screen effects (and insets), like superimposed shots, may be introduced effectively – but can degenerate too easily into visual gimmicks.

Long shots reveal overall pattern eg: intertwining movements and subgroup action, in dance, but cannot be sustained. Instead, we need closer shots of individuals – but these too have their problems. We may be on a group shot, and miss individual action, or·reach him just as he has finished. It can be difficult to isolate individuals. We may watch local action, and miss action elsewhere, or lose overall effect.

Where performers are static (bands, orchestras, groups) cameras must move around to the best possible vantage points (a *camera-tower* may help to get a higher viewpoint). But to get the right shot from the right position, at the right moment during continuous performance, is no mean feat. It requires careful attention to the score, precise planning, and skilled camerawork. Again, the principle of cover shots and cutting (or zooming) in to local action is used.

Pop music

Visually, anything goes, for the images aim to be different, to intrigue, amuse, astonish us. Pictures are often electronically doctored to create vibrant, multi-coloured images, distortions, colour conversions, etc., using chroma-key, colour synthesizer, off-monitor feedback effects (a camera shoots a monitor showing its own output).

Songs

Songs offer greater opportunity for varied visual treatment. In the *studio,* the singer may perform within a neutral setting such as a plain cyc, amidst decorative staging, abstract or associative, or an environmental background, a mock-up 'music room', perhaps . Shot on *location,* the singer miming to a tape playback, can walk beaches, row boats, or wander in gardens to suit the mood of the occasion. In a further approach, we hear the song to *associative pictures* on film, explored photographs – typically countryside, seascapes, snowscapes.

Close-ups
Close-ups of performers may be informative, but not particularly attractive.

High shots
High shots can reveal overall pattern and team formations.

Ground shots
Ground shots can show footwork, steps, swirling skirts.

Isolation
When shooting within a group it may be impossible to isolate individual performers so that unwanted items or people appear in shot.

Game Shows

Game shows are usually devised either as a contest between individuals, or competing teams. Contestants might be grouped behind a table unit, facing the 'quiz-master' at his desk. Sometimes participants take turns in answering questions and then unanswered items are thrown open to them all.

Layout and treatment
Shots should all be checked before the show, either with stand-ins or, preferably, by giving 'dummy questions' to contestants as a 'warm-up'.

Shots follow a pretty predictable pattern: *Quiz-master/chairman* (LS and MS); *panel* (group shot, individual close shots, 2-shots, reactions); *entrances/exits* of guests; *scoreboard shots*; shots of any *visual quiz material* (objects, graphics, slides, film clips); *audience shots*; *countdown clocks*, etc.

Panel games usually involve quite fast, adaptable shooting. Each cameraman is ready to provide his selected shots quickly and accurately. To aid identification, contestants have their names before them on the desk, together with indicators showing who is answering, or giving personal scores. A group shot helps in handling impromptu replies.

Organisation
In selecting questions for game shows, we need to make a carefully balanced choice between those that are too easy, and those that are too difficult – both for the contestants and for the audience. If we underestimate standards, it can lead to boredom and a tensionless performance. An over-estimate leaves people feeling inadequate, stupid, losing enthusiasm and interest. Questions must be clear, unambiguous, and their answers carefully checked beforehand – with any acceptable alternatives. It is widely agreed that questions should be rather easier at the start, to get the show under way.

The quiz master should have a friendly but firm manner, appearing totally impartial and in command. His answer cards and timing sheet help him to control running-time. If a studio audience is involved, he should have greeted them beforehand and given them any necessary guidance. This includes such remarks as: 'The mike can't pick up smiles, only applause and laughter . . . ' 'the FM will guide you so that we can transmit your enthusiasm, yet let the home audience hear the show'. At the start of the show, he outlines the rules, introduces competitors, and perhaps summarises the state of play of any previous programmes.

QUIZ SHOWS/PANEL GAMES

Typical shot allocation
Most quiz shows tend to follow a similar style-format. Consequently regular shooting-patterns develop. Where the contest is between two panels, with the chairman as adjudicator, the panel shots are duplicated.

The ultimate in sophisticated directing.

TV Drama

TV drama blends together the influences of script, performance, environmental effect, camerawork, editing, lighting and sound treatment.

Film and TV drama

Over simplifying, we can say that in film, emphasis is on action, activities and environment. Television studio drama more effectively depicts *re*-actions, with emphasis on character development, human relationships, discussion. The medium itself can embrace all aspects.

Because the TV screen is small and near, the TV viewer tends to scrutinise or inspect the picture. Cinema audiences have a greater sense of location and involvement, due to large-screen presentation. In TV, we can direct attention to specific detail, and give close-up emphasis, that in the cinema would appear grotesquely over-magnified.

TV drama technique

In TV studio drama, two fundamental methods are widely used. In the *semi-static* approach, cameras move around from their strategic positions to a relatively limited extent – normally zooming to modify shot-size. In the *dynamic* approach, camera viewpoints are mobile and continually varied. They follow action around, moving in amongst it with developing shots (page 92). The semi-static method is simpler, easier to plan and direct, and makes fewer demands on the production crew. But it too easily falls into a recognisable routine. Dynamic camerawork requires skilled operation and systematic planning.

Drama in the small studio

Begin by choosing simple concepts that you, the actors, and the system can handle. Analyse the script with facilities and available skills in mind. Ingenious effects that do not work, or draw attention to themselves, are best avoided. It would be better to play MACBETH against black drapes, or symbolic cyc-shadows, than use an unconvincingly crude 'cardboard' castle. Don't attempt to create replicas of complex environments. Use partial sets (page 137), chroma key (page 152), and similar economies, rather than provide inadequate, sparsely dressed staging.

Let your camera reveal the attitudes and reactions of characters. Do not give inexperienced actors too many moves or elaborate business. If they do not remember accurately, your shots and continuity will be lost. Inexperienced directors are liable to over-use close-ups, have excessive performer movement, or unduly static arrangements. Devise apparent *motivation* for moves (pages 80, 92), and get people into *naturalistic situations,* so that they look comfortable and purposeful. Avoid posed pictures, and moves that are so organised, you can almost hear actors reciting stage instructions. Give people location marks they can find easily, rather than have them looking for toe marks unnecessarily (page 118).

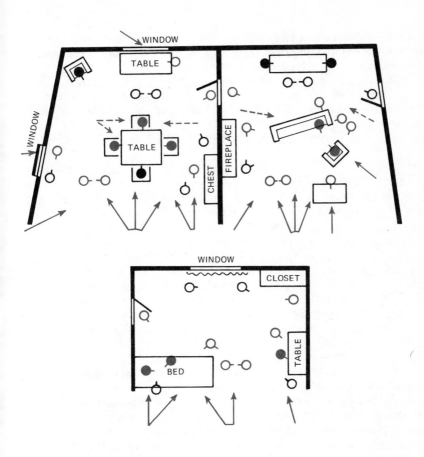

O— TYPICAL GOOD POSITION—STANDING	⟶ TYPICAL CAMERA POSITION
● TYPICAL GOOD POSITION—SITTING	⇢ POSSIBLE CAMERA POSITION
O—● POSITIONS RESTRICTING TREATMENT	

DRAMA

Basic room layouts for drama

The architecture and furnishing layouts of rooms directly influence the action-patterns and shot opportunities. Some positions offer better shots than others. Most action is central and downstage, taken on cross-shooting cameras. This provides maximum shot opportunity, and minimum audio and lighting difficulties.

Reminders on Effective Directing

Plan your show. Even a basic outline aids coordination.

Get very familiar with your script beforehand, so that it becomes a reference point, not a crutch.

Have firm ideas. Don't begin a rehearsal with vague hopes, or an expectation that it will be 'alright on the night'. Don't rely on multi-takes during videotaping, in a hope that eventual editing will cobble together a worthwhile production.

Welcome your guests, and ensure that they know what you want them to do.

Get to know your team beforehand. Don't just accept them as 'facilities'. Some directors call crew members by name, instead of by function. On balance, it prevents ambiguities to refer to 'Camera 1, Boom, Lighting' – particularly when they are all named Joe!

Always check that all the studio team, and contributors, eg: film, VTR, can hear talkback (intercom), and are ready to go.

Be consistent when using terms. Use local terminology.

Give clear guidance. Be decisive. Be firm but friendly, but don't order or browbeat. It does nothing but demoralise. Critical observations that are acceptable face-to-face, create tensions when heard over talkback (often without the opportunity to reply!).

Continually scrutinise preview monitors – Are shots O.K? Any guidance or changes needed? Have cameras moved to their next positions? Are graphics/titles ready and O.K?

Rehearse from the *production control room*. Don't keep going down to the studio to alter or correct. It wastes time, and concentration lapses. Most problems can be rectified from what you can see on camera, and with the aid of your FM and those members of the crew concerned.

Ensure that the crew knows which section you are about to rehearse (setting, shot number). If you are going over a section again, check that people realise why, and what was wrong last time.

Check at intervals on progress relative to available rehearsal time.

Don't leave items unrehearsed. Always check at the end of each section that the crew is ready to go on to the next.

Give preparatory standby to any source that has not been used for a long period, such as film inserts, or he may not be ready for immediate cueing.

Tell performers if they are creating problems, eg: he is shadowing her, or his hand is in the way. Don't assume they know, and will correct.

Some situations are not readily transformed by 'doctoring', eg: loud music cannot be faded down to make it a 'quiet background' behind commentary. A light-toned scene cannot be made to look dark by exposure or video adjustment (only by careful lighting treatment). Hence a daylight photograph cannot readily be transformed to 'night'. A dark-toned setting cannot be made to look light, however strongly lit.

If there is a delay during rehearsal because, for example, an item is not ready, pass on to another item, checking the linking between later.

After a rehearsal, have a short break to discuss with the performers, and the crew, if necessary any points to be corrected.

Be punctual. Don't be late starting rehearsal, time is precious. Don't leave people hanging about, waiting and wondering what to do. Always break at scheduled times such as meal breaks, and announce return times, and the point from which rehearsal will recommence.

Always be prepared to cope with a breakdown of facilities — particularly on live transmission — and anticipate possible alternative arrangements such as substituting another camera.

Do not over-rehearse — particularly amateur or inexperienced talent. It produces uncertainty, woodenness, less dynamic performances. Do not use time just because it's there. Under-rehearsal is equally undesirable.

After videotaping, hold the studio until the recording has been checked. If retakes are necessary, make this clear, and announce the sections and shot numbers involved, what was wrong, and the order of re-recording. Consider any costume/make-up/scenic changes necessary for the retakes.

At the end of transmission (taping) thank the crew and the performers. Be ready to praise work well done — but don't gush. They are professionals and know when they have done well or badly. A kind word oils the wheels of progress.

Check List – Common Errors

During rehearsal, the director is fully occupied with guiding and coordinating performers and crew. But all the time he remains alert to defects that can mar the impact of his production. Many will be dealt with by his various team specialists, but it is as well for the director to recognise the problems.

Performance errors
Unconvincing, 'wooden', 'mannered', out of character. Lines vary from script, parts missed. Positions, moves, business or timing wrong. Items handled incorrectly. Working to wrong camera. Voice too loud, or quiet. Self-conscious. Fidgety. Inconsistent. Off marks. Late on cue.

Camera errors
Unsharp focus. Focused on wrong subject (or plane). Losing focus. Missed shots. Wrong shot. Poor composition (wrong framing or headroom, subject cut-off). Composition not as rehearsed. Camera off its marks. Unsteady camera work (or zoom). Poor subject-following. Wrong camera height. Lens flares. Wrong lens angle. Caught readjusting (height, zoom change, focus change) in shot. Shooting off.

Lighting
Too flat (unmodelled results). Too contrasty (over-dramatic). Important subjects or areas cannot be seen. Areas too bright. Ineffective light direction (wrong angle, too steep). Unattractive pictorial effect. Distracting reflections. Distracting shadows (of camera, mike or boom) on people or settings or of people on to people, or background. Unattractive portraiture. Excess backlight. Poor environmental illusion. Poor pictorial continuity between shots.

Staging
Unconvincing. Inappropriate. Lacks visual appeal. Not suitable in shots used eg: ineffective in close shots or provides overall effect not seen by camera. Only suitable from certain viewpoints. Effective in colour, but not monochrome. Identical effect could have been achieved more easily or cheaply. Staging inhibits production treatment eg: camera movement, lighting, sound. Surface tones unsuitable (too light, dark, shiny).

Video control ('Racks', 'Shading')
Highlights too bright. Shadows too thin dense (set/sat up or down). Contrast excessive or inadequate. Successive pictures poorly matched (in colour, brightness).

Film inserts
Poor match to studio (picture quality, continuity, sound). Distracting blemishes. Sound out of sync (voice not timed to lip movements).

176

Slides
Poor quality (bad colour, blemishes, unsharp). Wrongly aligned.

Titles
Inappropriate type-face. Lettering too large or small. Positioning in frame unsuitable. Wrongly aligned. Consecutive slides unmatched. Unsuitable tone or contrast.

Audio
No sound. Opening or closing words or notes missed (late fade in or early fade out). Unwanted material heard (early fade in or late fade out). Wrong mike (wrong source; performer sounds distant, off-mike background sounds too loud). Poor balance (inappropriate relative volumes; sound scale/proportions do not match picture). Inappropriate acoustics eg: reverberation in open air shot. Extraneous studio noises (hum, ventilation or equipment noise). Rumble of wind on mike, camera cable drag noise, rustles, crackles (costume, script noise), staging-movement noise (moving props, altering settings). Mike phasing (fading, distortion, bass loss). Howlround or feedback (hollow, reverberant, even oscillating sound). Audio cues badly timed eg: audio disc or tape insert late or early. Slur, or wow, on run-up of recorded insert (cueing or operational error). Sound effects (do not match picture). Unsatisfactory quality (incorrect tonal balance or distortion). Audio chain defects (clicks, crackles, hum, tape drop-out and speed fluctuations).

Studio Audience

Unquestionably, certain productions gain appreciably from the presence of a studio audience. Comedy shows in particular, lose their 'edge' when played 'cold' to the camera. Even an appreciative camera crew's reactions can help.

Controlling the audience

Various audience conventions have evolved. At concerts, for example, we expect our audience to be silent except for subsequent applause, hopefully not coughing, fidgeting, or reacting audibly. In 'situation comedy' shows (comedy action in realistic settings) we want to *hear* the audience laughing and clapping throughout, but not whistling or giving inaudible smiles. They are not seen on camera, though, for this would disrupt the 'real-life' presentation. Because long laughter can slow down the show, upsetting timing, the FM diplomatically but firmly encourages and terminates audience reactions. He, or the director, has explained this need during the welcoming *warm-up* before the show with smiles, jokes, or other encouragement. Some studios use applause signs. Others introduce recorded applause, usually during editing/dubbing sessions afterwards, to augment or substitute for the audience. Directors argue that although recordings may seem unethical, and often sound phoney, at least they are controllable!

Effect on performers

Some directors contend that talent can time their laughs and business better to a studio audience but others feel that the tempo slows, relative to the home viewers' more rapid reactions. When talent is unused to TV work, they are more inclined to 'address' the audience, or use a 'stagey' delivery, instead of the more confidential, intimate approach that is more suitable for TV. We may find our studio audience reacting to events that the camera is not yet showing (a clown awaiting his entrance). This can puzzle and frustrate the home viewer. Studio audiences are also liable to over-react, due to group enthusiasm, determination to enjoy themselves, and a rather less critical attitude than the isolated viewer.

Accommodating the audience

As well as providing comfortable, safe seating, we must ensure that our audience can see the studio action clearly. So sets have to be arranged facing them, slung picture monitors and loudspeakers helping them follow the television treatment. When audiences actually participate in the show, cameramen normally offer reaction shots, that the director intercuts with the front-of-camera (or on-camera) material. But if people see themselves on monitors, we must be prepared for giggles, shy and extrovert behaviour. Self-consciousness ruins reaction shots.

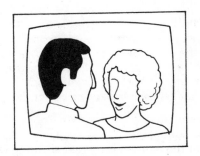

STUDIO AUDIENCE

Studio audience viewpoint
The studio audience watches a performance under intriguingly unfamiliar
conditions, with distracting mechanics all round.   1. Foldback loudspeaker.
2. Picture monitor. The viewer sees nothing of the behind-the-scenes activities,
and is quite oblivious to them, seeing only a naturalistic, 'real-life' situation.
The various floor operations (eg: close cameras) should not obscure the action
from the studio audience.

On Location

The problems and opportunities when shooting on location alter with the show and whether we are shooting inserts or a complete production.

The 'recce' (site reconnaissance) location scouting

Success begins with efficient site reconnaissance – the 'recce'. Anticipation at this stage can prevent many headaches later. Preliminary investigations of potential sites are later followed up by the director and his specialist team.

Interiors: Typical considerations include – space available (small rooms restrict the longest shot possible), potential shots, viewpoint restrictions, acoustics and extraneous noises, view outside windows. While interiors are sheltered from the weather, they invariably need lighting, as natural light proves inadequate. The interior may need dressing (drapes, furniture, props), and even to be modified by scenic additions eg: introducing a false door or pillar.

Exteriors; Here we also have a number of factors that are in the lap of the gods, including weather (raining, windy, or cold), light conditions (bright and contrasty, dull and overcast or failing light). Will the chosen area be in shade at the time of shooting? Will strong winds create rumble on mike? Are local extraneous noises, (traffic, aircraft, animals, machinery, etc.) liable to be troublesome? Are there incongruities visible (high tension pylons which mar an 'historical scene')?

Much depends on the size and spread of the area involved. Localised action clearly presents fewer problems than widespread movement. A walk in the open may use natural light, augmented perhaps, while a similar interior walk may necessitate extensive lighting.

Organisation

One needs to take a very practical approach to location work. Apart from obtaining appropriate permissions for shooting, assessing vehicle access, problems with terrain, congestion, parking, crowd control, accommodation, feeding and weather shelter, other requirements must be anticipated. It is as well to have clear ideas too, on union rules re: manning (crew size), overtime, etc.

Although it may be possible to return to base for supplies, much time is saved by selecting items to make the going smoother – from walkie-talkies and loud-hailers, to materials for improvisation. Self-reliance and accurate estimation of needs are the watchwords!

To forestall later difficulties, we shall often shoot more than one version of an action (straight retakes, or with variations), together with *wild tracks* (unsynchronised background sounds) to provide flexibility for later editing and dubbing. Continuity checks are essential, using photo record shots if the studio action, costume, make-up, lighting, setting, has to match the location shooting.

WEATHER

SOUND

Acoustics
Noise

Predictability
Shelter
Precautions
Alternative shooting

TERRAIN FEATURES

Required
Spurious
Undesirable

SERVICE CRAFTS

Make-up
Wardrobe
Lighting
Scenic

ENVIRONMENT

LIGHT

Intensity
Contrast
Direction
Duration

REGULATIONS

Police
Local authority
Union rules
Permission
Crowd control
Congestion

TRANSPORT

Road access
Parking
Travel time

POWER SUPPLIES

Local
Supplementary
Cabling problems

FACILITIES

ECONOMICS

Costing/Budget
Schedules

SUPPLIES BACK-UP

Materials
Equipment
Labour

PEOPLE

Transport of.
Catering
Accommodation
Dressing/changing facilities
Intercommunication

CHECK FACILITIES

Local Videotape
Film checks

ON LOCATION

Location considerations
In evaluating a location, a variety of factors must be considered. Not only is its artistic suitability important, but the many practical facets of a complex operation must also be taken into account.

Colour TV

Colour can not make a poorly directed production good, but it can extend the range of subjects that we can show effectively.

Does colour affect directing?
Attitudes vary. Some directors say, 'Methods are the same as before but now it's in colour'. As we'll see, this can be a naive misjudgement. Others want to 'explore colour in all its glory'. This can lead to an over-prominence of colour, to distracting, inappropriate use – with no evident effect for the monochrome viewer.

The ways the human eye and brain interpret the world of colour, differ appreciably from the responses of TV and film cameras. Situations that are acceptable to the eye often have a different impact on the screen. We can have strong psychological reactions to colours that appear to be adjacent in the picture – although in reality one is located on a plane far behind the other. Facial tones can be modified considerably by background hues. Furthermore, many colours are strongly associative, and influence how we feel about what we see. The frame that encloses the picture can make the colour of the scene appear more intense than in real life. We judge colour from experience, but in a somewhat arbitrary fashion. We accept inaccurate skin tones but strongly criticise the reproduction of favorite flowers.

Colour brings opportunities
Colour has eye-appeal. Whoever went into raptures over a monochrome sunset? Colour can create mood, arrest interest, direct attention. It can clarify detail, differentiate between planes that would merge in monochrome. Colour can be subtle (desaturated, pastel hues) or it can be blatant (pure, saturated hues). Colour brings great opportunities for staging, costumes, lighting, visual display.

But colour brings problems!
Remember that some people at home are still watching monochrome pictures, so always check the impact of the shot in black-and-white, particularly for graphics. Colour easily becomes garish, brash, trashy, and cheapens visual appeal. Scenes can look too colourful or cosy – even when we are showing squalor. While defocused objects merge in monochrome, they can become frustratingly indecipherable in colour. Superimposed colours mix to form different, often unrealistic effects. Coloured objects can dominate, even when they are intended as supporting or background items. Cutting rates in colour tend to be slower. Colour matching between shots can be quite difficult. But between different sources such as slides, film, photographs, it is often impossible. Colour needs care. At its best it adds another dimension to the director's opportunities.

182

Natural light
Natural light can be analysed into a spectrum of hues.

Colour analysis
It has been found that this colour range can be reproduced by using mixtures of red, green, and blue light. The TV camera scans the coloured scene, analysing it into these components. The three separate video signals *(chrominance),* together with a component corresponding with the 'brightness' of each part of the shot *(luminance),* may require one, two, three or four TV pick-up tubes in the camera.

TV systems
This information has to be specially coded for transmission, and subsequently decoded at the receiver. Three incompatible coding systems are in use.

Colour mixtures
As well as the three primary colours (red, green, blue), there are the three secondary or complementary hues — yellow, cyan (blue-green), and magenta (red-blue) — that come from mixing the primaries.

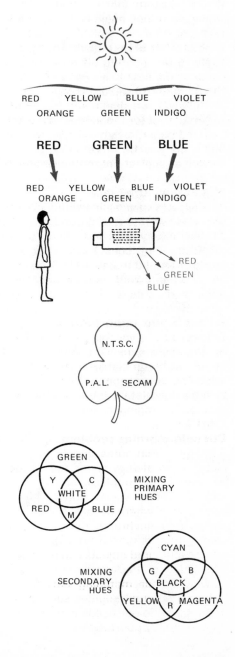

RED   YELLOW   BLUE   VIOLET
ORANGE   GREEN   INDIGO

RED   GREEN   BLUE

RED   YELLOW   BLUE   VIOLET
ORANGE   GREEN   INDIGO

RED
GREEN
BLUE

N.T.S.C.

P.A.L.   SECAM

GREEN
Y   C
WHITE
RED   M   BLUE

MIXING PRIMARY HUES

CYAN
G   B
BLACK
YELLOW   R   MAGENTA

MIXING SECONDARY HUES

183

Appendix – Calculating Shots

If we want to plan a production systematically and predictably, a transparent lens-angle (or protractor) laid on the *scale staging plan* is a fast and effective technique (pages 102–3). It shows us at a glance, exactly what we are going to see from any viewpoint, whether we are likely to be shooting off or getting another camera in shot. As we go through the scene, we can mark the camera positions on the plan as a record for eventual rehearsals.

However, we shall meet occasions where we need the solution to an isolated problem, and do not want to resort to measurements on squared paper. This graph can help with its summarised information. It will show you the lens angle and distance needed for any standard shot, as well as subject proportions in the frame.

How to use the graph
1. Follow a vertical line from your camera distance to the lens angle in use, and *the shot you obtain* is shown on the left.
2. Similarly, you can see *how far away* the camera needs to be for a particular shot. Locate your shot on the left, follow across to the lens angle used, and the distance is below.
3. What *lens angle* is necessary for a shot? A horizontal line from the shot type, joins a vertical from camera distance, at the lens angle needed.
4. The scene *width and height taken in* are shown in the left-hand column, so you can see camera distances required for various captions.
5. *Proportions,* too, are shown. If a subject is to occupy one-third of the screen width (or height), multiply its actual width (or height) by three (or whatever proportion is involved), and use the vertical width scale to deduce the distance for your lens angle.

Lens angles
The corresponding horizontal and vertical angles covered are;

Horizontal	5	8	10	12	16	18	20	24	30	35	38	40	45	50	55°
Vertical	$3\frac{3}{4}$	6	$7\frac{1}{2}$	9	12	$13\frac{1}{2}$	15	18	$22\frac{1}{2}$	26	$28\frac{1}{2}$	30	34	$37\frac{1}{2}$	41°

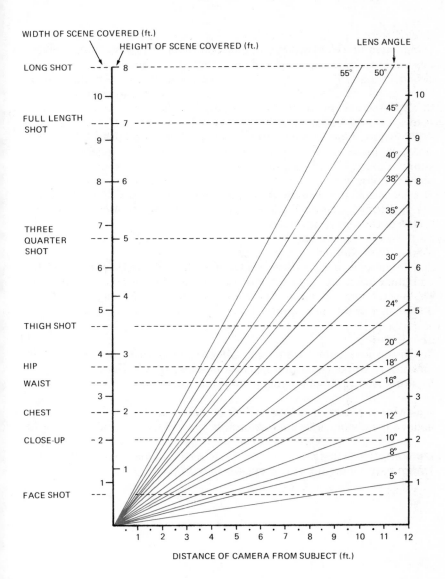

WIDTH OF SCENE COVERED (ft.)

HEIGHT OF SCENE COVERED (ft.)

LENS ANGLE

DISTANCE OF CAMERA FROM SUBJECT (ft.)

UNIVERSAL CAMERA SET-UP GRAPH

The graph shows direction and staging details that would otherwise need continual measurement. It is calibrated in feet, but can be interpreted in inches. To use it for greater distances multiply the scale readings by a similar factor (eg ×5).

185

Further Reading

BRETZ, Rudy:
Techniques of Television Production. McGraw-Hill, New York. Includes descriptions of equipment and production methods used in the TV studio.

CHESTER, G., GARRISON, G. R., WILLIS, E. E.:
Television and Radio. Appleton-Century-Crofts, Meredith Corpn., New York. Includes useful summaries of productional organisation, facilities and techniques.

LEWIS, Colby:
The TV Director/Interpreter. Hastings House, New York. 'A guide to help TV directors translate the meaning of their programmes through the media of cameras and microphones'.

MILLERSON, Gerald:
The Technique of Television Production. Focal Press/Hastings House. A comprehensive study of the mechanics, techniques and aesthetics of TV production, including detailed analysis of picture composition, editing and production approaches.

ZETTL, Herbert:
Television Production Handbook. Wadsworth Publishing Co. Inc., Belmont, California. A useful survey of specific television equipment, together with production applications, usage and organisation.

The Media Manuals series includes a number of specially designed volumes covering specific aspects of the Television and Film media. These provide introductory texts for students, specialists, managerial staff, educationalists, on such subjects as TV camerawork, TV staging, TV lighting, TV sound, studio design, film processing, etc.

Glossary

Acting Area (56) Action region within a setting.
Ad lib (96) Unrehearsed, unscripted action or speech.

Background (56, 60, 109, 112, 136, 152, 182) *(Scenic)* Areas appearing behind a subject. *(Audio)* Holding the volume (level) of music and effects down, to make dialogue more prominent. *(Programme research)* The underlying facts; information on which programme material is based.
Backing (Protection) (57, 95) Scenic planes beyond windows, doors, etc., that prevent the camera seeing unwanted areas outside the setting.
Backing Copy (Protection Copy) (150) Duplicate recording; in case main copy becomes damaged.
Backlight (59) Light directed towards the camera.
Balance (50, 54, 58) Adjustment of relative sound volumes (levels), or light intensities for artistically satisfying effect. *Pictorial balance* similarly relates to the distribution of line and tonal masses.
Bloom (Block Off, Crush Out, Burn Out) (60, 64, 176) Excessively light surface, reproducing as blank white area.
Blow-Up Greatly enlarged photograph.
Boom, Sound (50, 52, 53, 60, 101) A fixed or telescopic arm on a wheeled stand, supporting a slung microphone.
Burn In, (Burn On) (176) An image of a bright area retained (temporarily or permanently) on a camera-tube, defacing subsequent pictures.
Busy (71) An over-decorated, complicated, or elaborate effect.

Camera Tower (18, 168) Scaffolding tower, supporting TV camera for high shots.
Camera Trap (61) Opening specially arranged within scenery (eg: sliding panel, hinged wall-picture, shutters) through which a concealed camera can shoot.
Caption Scanner (Slide Chain) (146) Apparatus for televising slides, sometimes small cards – titles, artwork, photographs ('telop', or 'balop').
Cast (144) Performers seen and heard in a production. Hence *cast list.*
Chain (12, 13) General term for a complete assembly of technical equipment with a specific function; eg: audio chain – from microphone to loudspeaker. Camera chain – from camera to picture monitor or receiver.
Clip (121) Short section excerpted from a film or VTR programme; usually to become an *insert* into another. *Also* to inadvertently omit a note, syllable, or word from the start or end of an audio sequence (late or premature fade or cut).

Closed Circuit (124) Not transmitted/broadcast. A programme fed (distributed) to limited, selected points.

Contrast (58) Relative 'brightness' of lightest and darkest tones.

Costing (69) Cost assessment of materials, equipment, manpower, etc.

Crane (71) Special type of camera dolly with a jib (boom, crane) arm raising camera and cameraman to an appreciable height – eg: 7–25ft.). *Also 'to crane'* is to move the jib up/down.

Credits Names of production personnel, cast, at the start/end of a programme.

Crop, to To cut off, eg: shot framed to omit subjects near its borders.

Cross-Shot (40, 86) Oblique camera viewpoint.

Cushion (166) Potentially expendable subject matter in a production, that can be shortened or cut to adjust overall duration.

Cutaway (34, 48, 95, 142, 158) A separate shot interposed within a main action sequence (eg: a crowd shot, during a football game) to deliberately interrupt its continuity. This enables boring, lengthy or incomplete material to be edited relatively unobtrusively.

Dead Not (or no longer) to be used. Unwanted. 'Killed'. Not functioning.

Defocus Mix (46) A transition between two shots, in which the first camera defocuses during the mix, while the second sharpens on its shot.

Depth of Field (23, 27, 30, 33, 42, 109) Distance range over which the scene appears sharp. Increases with smaller lens aperture/stop (needs greater light intensity), and as lens angle is increased (scene appears more distant; perspective distortion).

Dolly (18, 34) Small wheeled platform supporting a tripod, extensible column, or movable jib arm, to which the camera panning head and camera head are fitted. The dolly provides flexibility of camera movement and position, and requires several operators. The term 'dolly' is loosely used for any mobile mounting.

Dress, to (56) To wear the clothes to be used during the recording/transmission (ie: for *Dress run*). *Also* to arrange set dressings (furniture, drapes, etc.) in position.

Dubbing (150) Recording an existing recording (audio or video).

Duplex, Multiplex A facility for enabling a single static unit or equipment chain (TV camera) to be re-routed to any of several different sources (eg: film, slide, captions).

Establishing Shot (34, 84) Overall shot revealing environment and positions, at the start of a scene.

Elevations (57, 101) Drawings giving the dimensions and details of vertical planes (eg: walls: with doors, windows, pillars, surface treatment, etc.).

188

Favour, to To give greater prominence to one person than another.

Feed (14) Supply. Hence to *'feed* a monitor with Cam. 2's picture'.

Flat (101) Scenic unit (in various standard sizes), made from a wooden frame faced with plywood, compressed board, or canvas. Mainly used to form 'walls' of settings, and vertical planes.

Floor Men (Stage Hands, Grips) (11) Studio crew who erect (set up), dress, and dismantle (strike) scenery. Perhaps also handling captions, moving props/scenery during the show.

Floor Plan (100, 101, 102, 173) Scale bird's-eye view of the layout of the studio (staging, furniture, cameras, etc., being added progressively).

Fly, to To suspend scenery or objects.

Foldback Studio loudspeakers used to play music/effects into the studio.

Freeze frame (150) A single film or VTR frame held or repeated to arrest motion.

Frontal Shot Camera viewpoint straight-on to action.

Hard Focus (36) Sharply focused.

Helical Scanning (150) A videotape system using single or dual heads to scan the tape (slant track).

Hot (50, 52, 53, 60, 101) Overbright surface. Equipment that is working, e.g. 'hot mike'.

Kill (186) Eliminate, cut out.

Lavaliere (51) Small mike hung round the neck on a cord.

Limbo (172) Strictly, a totally black background for action. Has come to indicate a neutral or unrecognisable background.

Line-Up Technical adjustment of equipment to provide optimum performance (particularly of camera channels). Circuit checks, alignment, etc.

Live (14, 54) Direct transmission of action as it happens. *(Audio).* Reverberant.

Live-on-Tape A show videorecorded in its entirety, without stops or editing.

Loop A length of film or audio tape, in which the ends are joined to permit continuous repeated performance, (eg: identifying announcements), or a continuous effect (eg: rain, fog).

Lose the Light, to The moment when a camera's tally (cue) light goes off – ie: when the director has switched to another video source – often used to indicate to a camera when to move to another position.

M and E Music and effects only. Sound track without speech or dialogue.

Magnetic (Mag) Track A magnetic sound recording (single or multi-track) on a standard sprocketed film base. *Sep-mag.* – a separate such recording, run in-sync with the mute picture print. *Magnetic stripe* in which the sound track is laid alongside the edge of the film, combines in one 'married' or 'combined' print both the picture and its sound.

Master Control Switching and continuity centre to which various programme sources are fed.

Minimum Focusing Distance (32) The shortest distance from the camera at which objects can still be focused.

Mirror Shot (89) Picture in which the camera shoots a subject via a mirror, rather than by pointing at it directly.

Over-Shoulder Shot (41, 79, 84, 159, 160) Shooting over the shoulder of a foreground person.

P.D. (Public Domain) Non-copyright material, that can be performed without permission or payment.

Parallel (Platform, Rostrum) (101) Horizontal platform on wooden or tubular frame.

Pick Ups (Buffer Shots) Extra material filmed or telerecorded, to serve as cutaway shots, and facilitate editing.

Playback (149) To reproduce audio or videotape for check purposes; usually immediately after recording.

Practical (56) Working; scenic features (eg: doors), models, etc., as opposed to non-practical (not functioning) properties.

Props (Properties) (56) Articles used to decorate settings, eg: vases, books, furniture, etc. *Personal props* are items specifically used or worn by actors.

Public Address Loudspeaker system relaying announcements/music to an audience.

Quadruture (quad) scanning (150) A videotape system using a rotating four-headed scanning mechanism.

Rear Projection (Back Projection) A translucent screen onto which film or slides are projected from behind, and shot by cameras on the front side.

Reflex Projection Front projection along the lens axis, onto a finely beaded screen, to provide a scenic background.

Reverse Action (150) Action made to appear backwards in time sequence.

Reverse Shot (48) Shot from the opposite direction to a previous viewpoint.

Riser (Block) Small wooden block or platform (various sizes) used to support furniture and small items, for display, or to build out standard platforms (parallels, rostra).

Roller Caption (Crawl) (144) Titling on a long paper strip (usually black), rolled through the camera's shot.

Segue (Pronounced Seg-Way) Where one piece of music, effects, dialogue, cross-fades into another, often imperceptibly (fade-out of one source during the fade-in of the next). (Sometimes misused, for 'sneak-in'.)

Set, to (56) To put into the required/rehearsed position. At the end of a rehearsal, props, furniture, etc., are re-set in their opening positions.

Shot Box (16) TV camera push-button facility permitting automatic readjustment of zoom lens to specific angles; often at pre-set speed.

Sit (Bat Down, Batting Down on Blacks, sat or set down) Crushing the darkest tones in the picture to an even black.

Sneak In (or Out) To introduce (or remove) imperceptibly, unobtrusively.

Soft Focus (36) Unsharp (accidentally, or deliberately for artistic effect). Opposite of 'hard focus'.

Split Focus (36, 42) Focusing so that chosen subjects, at different distances from the camera, are equally sharply focused (distributing the depth of field).

Spread (124) To take more than allotted/anticipated time.

Stage Brace (57) Extensible prop or stay used to hold up scenery.

Staging Area (Sound Stage, Stage) (12) Main area of studio floor, in which staging may be arranged. It is surrounded by a safety area (fire lane), from which staging is normally prohibited.

Stretch (115, 124) To slow down, to take more time.

Strike Removal of scenery, props, etc., from a setting.

Studio Address/Loudspeaker Talkback The use of a loudspeaker to address studio performers/staff. (In US also termed *talkback*.)

Superimpose (Super) (46) Two or more video sources transmitted simultaneously; creating a transparent effect only where a lighter tone in one coincides with darker areas in another.

Telecine (13, 121) Equipment chain for televising film (film island).

Throw Away To underplay a dramatic opportunity, either accidentally, or for deliberate effect.

Thrown, to Be (118) To be distracted, interrupting one's performance.

Tight (124) Without surplus space around subject. Running too close to allotted duration to permit spread.

Time Check (120) Synchronizing clocks to ensure simultaneous starts.

Tracking Shot (Dolly Shot) (28) Extensive dolly movement; particularly when following alongside moving performer in a constant-size shot.

Video Control (Shading) (12, 14) Continual adjustment of video equipment (exposure, black level, video gain, gamma, colour balance), to maintain optimum picture quality and match picture sources, by the Video engineer/vision operator/shader.

Walk on, a A non-speaking performance.

Whip Pan (Zip Pan) (38, 94) Rapid panning movement, showing the scene clearly focused at the start and end of panning, with intermediate blurring.

Winging a Show (96) Unrehearsed direction.

Wipe (Magnetic) (148) To demagnetise a magnetic recording (audio or video).

Wipe (Visual) (44, 46, 47, 66) Visual effect in which the existing picture is progressively replaced by part(s) of another.